# What Light Can Do

Also by Luke Whitington and published by Ginninderra Press
*Only Fig & Prosciutto*

Luke Whitington

# What Light Can Do
## New & Collected Poems

## Thanks to

Mark O'Connor
Theodore Ell
Bernard Hardy
Ann McGarrell
Richard Hugo
Antonia Hoddle
Geoff Page
Paolo Totaro
Les Murray
Barry Spurr
Mark Tredinnick

*What Light Can Do*
ISBN 978 1 76109 351 7
Copyright © text Luke Whitington 2022
Cover design: Julian Canny

First published 2022 by
**GINNINDERRA PRESS**
PO Box 3461 Port Adelaide 5015
www.ginninderrapress.com.au

# Contents

| | |
|---|---:|
| Preface | 9 |

## I What Light Can Do

| | |
|---|---:|
| Talking to leaves | 15 |
| Sunlight | 17 |
| Shapes of quietness | 18 |
| Bobundara | 19 |
| Towards another summer | 21 |
| A human weathervane | 23 |
| Indifferent skies | 24 |
| A wounded splendour | 27 |
| Driving to cicadas | 29 |
| Pagan moon | 30 |
| Cascade | 32 |
| Return to the silence | 34 |
| Embers to ashes | 36 |
| Still, not yet forever | 38 |
| Dust and time | 39 |
| What light can do | 40 |
| Green silence | 43 |
| Land's dialectics | 44 |
| Unlit window | 47 |
| The old place | 50 |
| Her coiled blue curves | 52 |
| The rock pool | 54 |
| Magic and sunshine | 56 |
| The woman walks | 58 |
| Bunyah | 59 |
| Ashes of silence | 61 |
| Heaney's wind | 63 |

| | |
|---|---|
| Once a Swedish poet | 64 |
| The man without leaves | 65 |
| The friend who flew away | 67 |
| A cliff of sky between the birds | 68 |
| Wind with a different destination | 70 |
| Shadows of journeys | 71 |
| Absences | 73 |
| Pebbles and memory | 76 |
| The Kiss | 78 |
| Beach boy | 79 |
| A shadow's discourse | 80 |
| The sight of lost time | 82 |
| September in Renaissance Italy | 84 |
| Season aslant | 86 |
| Letter to a friend, in Florence | 88 |
| Aphrodite? | 90 |

## II Breathless in Exile

| | |
|---|---|
| Breathless in exile | 93 |
| Ikos | 95 |
| The poet in exile | 97 |
| The swallows in Saint Peter's Square | 100 |
| Expatriate | 101 |
| A chunk of heaven | 103 |
| Juggling Italian | 107 |
| Polgeto, a village of Umbria | 109 |
| Torte al testo | 111 |
| August in Rome | 113 |
| Umbrian moon | 117 |
| A fountain, casting moments of time | 119 |
| Ruins | 122 |
| Whether or not to love a tree | 124 |

| | |
|---|---|
| Far from the city | 127 |
| Islands and their ruins | 129 |
| Venus in Rome | 131 |
| The bar on the Lungarno | 133 |
| Lunch in Napoli | 135 |
| Venetian idyll | 137 |
| The Naked Lunch | 140 |
| Bologna | 142 |
| Exile – Or a crossroad in the realms of youth? | 144 |
| Nardia | 146 |
| Piazza delle Signoria: the square of the lords | 147 |
| Return to the hills and the Tuscan plain | 148 |
| Perpetual midday | 151 |
| Central park and Columbus Avenue | 152 |
| Cappuccino and almond cake | 154 |
| A smile in Italian | 156 |
| The little waves | 160 |
| Remembering Lerici | 163 |
| Driftwood | 164 |
| A room fallen asleep | 165 |
| In memory of Basil | 166 |
| Bells I can remember – Venice | 168 |
| Praying aloud | 170 |
| The man in the Academia | 171 |
| Venice, summer ends | 173 |
| Acknowledgements | 175 |

# Preface

A preface cannot pretend to elucidate a volume of poems. It is for the poems to illuminate themselves but it is a poet who enables this. Luke has a gift for bringing pasts into clearly focused and felt images of time conditioned life states, meetings, events, loves among its ruins, refreshed worlds, what poets are for.

Consciousness is a compound of recent sensory inputs, memories and archival pop-up shreds of recollections, all of which constitute our sense of the present. Our constructs of the realities we individually conceive derive from this mass of data which is continually renewed by ongoing experiences which interactions modify our earlier conceptions of ourselves. Our idea of a 'now', an immediate sense of being, is made up of bytes of personal and inherited remembered experiences. Last year is always part of right now.

Memory for Luke Whitington's is his life's existential continuum. At times he is Proustian in his resurrections of lost time, at other times he brings to mind Cavafy's search for his Ithaca. Memory is the space of Luke's timescapes where he lingers in the personal world of female companionship; walks by diners gesturing at a table in a piazza or records in the silence of his hotel room reflections on a classical past as it contrasts with a recent, more vital event, which he transmutes into poetic form. His poems are haunted by pasts as they weave in and out of his contexts of fleshed-out figuration contrasted with classical stone statuary or a seagull from Ostia ghosting a dark, empty town square, nature alive and well surviving the memorial antiquity of an emperor's head which now serves as the bird's perch.

So the poet realises in his sensographics a collaging of many conceptual states and moods to a point where his poems become almost post-temporal dimensions in their reach for a compounding of past and present. When he draws together a sunlit beach with voiceless streets, the coupling defeats articulation and a stanza fades into 'a darkness of words', a blackout perhaps of something once felt intensely that defies regeneration, a redacted reality.

> Idling on some Liguria beach
> Green eyes squinting at the sea, a swarthy Venus
> Getting cocoa-brown all over
> Shapely mythology ensconced in a tangerine bikini
> Here in streets that have lost their tongue
> You grapple with a darkness of words
>
> from 'August in Rome'

It is Luke's grasp of his role as summoner of the done and dusted to support the stagecraft of contemporary being that expresses his attention to his role as director in the plays he produces in his poems. Emanator of expressions of his personal existential condition, he reveals in his writing his insights into the mind-worlds we build from memories and their preludes, our calls to action. Let's leave the last lines of this preface to the poet.

> Ancient history drifts over blazing waters
> Then the show goes out, late walkers
> Striding alone, metronomes of steps in narrow alleys
> High tide barely whispering, a slow languid
> lapping – you stop again under a Romeo and Juliet balcony
> It's all the same, the old abandoned stage

Why do you return? The view will never be new
It is serenely the same, everything here
From monument to paving stone, waits
To be seen again. Is there a motive undiscovered –
Why frequent, why haunt this place? – You walk on
                    from 'A chunk of heaven'

                                Bernard Hardy

# I

# What Light Can Do

# Talking to leaves

Poplars like tall, keeling masts
Shedding golden flakes in their wake
I drive with a tailwind of leaves
Scattering, tumbling down the road of my past
Memories shrink to the rear-vision view
The road behind in sympathy
Moves like a wounded tail, twitching from side to side.
These beautiful trees have accepted their destiny
So must I, sailing the road, westward recklessly.

I was mostly fair I remember, I made sure
I made use of false and true
In equal measures – and nothing dear one, is true forever.
Sometimes my love poems were really elegies
But love, sweet thing, is a death of sorts.

Leaves floating past like wood spirits
Road veering outwards now, shouldering into the bigger view
The distant mountains slurring into smudged blue haze
Visions, illusions dance in the air, I remember the best
From a dubious past; girls who had the misfortune
To place faith in me; someone born to be a loner

A loser mostly; lazing inside my quietly spoken but false persona –
The forgotten may curse me
For triggering, encouraging, their curiosity
Left standing there now, outside the footlights of memory –
I drive on, with my stiff, convinced smile, foolishly
Down the road of my heart's old ruthlessness
Nothing or nobody can save me now –

I laugh at the plane leaves – impishly
Clutching the wind (hope?) with open autumnal hands
Leaping across the bonnet and windscreen –
Is it a kind of warning? Nature's one last try? – But I will ignore this
For sure, as I know I'm doomed to go down with the ship
Talking to leaves and changing gears
Laughing in the mirror like a lunatic.

# Sunlight

Sunlight could recount
A story or two
A burglar streaming through
My window, stealing

Life from a pine table
Drying nutrients, milking
An open dictionary
Erasing a half-written draft

Altering meanings
And disappearing in the evening
Leaving bleached sentences behind –
Shadows not sunlight

Help my imagining
Borrowing and returning moments
Brushing the light away to one side –
Swallowing the present, immediate things.

Dust of memory
Bears my fingerprints
Where outlines remain
As guilty as sunlight.

# Shapes of quietness

For Trisha Dixon

She called and said – come
And see my country – so I did, I drove
Through high forests
On the back roads

Then down; a long glide descending
Into her plains, her loping grey
Formations of land; treeless, naked
Brooding landscape

Sensual looping, pooling shapes of silence –
On a crest I stopped; sat in the idling
Car and watched the sunset;
The flood of yellow; a sea of fading fire –

And then I drove on down, to find
On a curve, her unnamed gate –
I had come to find a woman's laughter
Sunlit chuckling waters

In her voice – yet I found two –
Instead of one – Monaro
In her shapely quiet
Had gifted me, two dusk-lit smiles.

# Bobundara

Driving Monaro
Driving April toward scents of snow
I did not follow the curving road
Downward, slowing – wind ahead carrying dust away

Instead I turned
Through the unnamed gate; stopped and looked –
Silence brooding over the treeless plain
Beneath the hills something of some presence left

Only the softened, turning curves remembered –
Below – Bobundara; the long veranda waiting
Poplar leaves falling with a languid flame's grace
And seated around the long table

Many of those who lived those moments –
A sense of turning, reaching, speaking, being
In History repeated; Lunch in the old dining room;
Walls of hand-bound books watching over us – all those who remember

Taking a place in a page remained of unfaded time
Time falling through portraits
And photographs, time mellowed on papered walls
Time watching from eyes framed in corridors –

And the talk went on with gusto, the wine
A kindly, loquacious friend
And the crust of roasted smashed potatoes
And the salmon and the dark sweet berries
Savoured with what was remembered;

A profile, a smile, a little girl's first party dress
The blur of a head dancing, turning past –
Stories of stoic pastoral centuries
The emigrations of golden pastures –

And heavens turning circles of wayward light away.

The joyous reunions and some painful separations
The journeys started in far away places
That criss-crossed all their way to here –
Finally here at this happily, groaning table

Surrounded by gathered words, the gilded covers climbing
Shelves into a softer light, the laughter swirling on past
The raised glasses; the books becoming jealous
Of so many words; the swirling brook of talk at Bobundara

Sweeping and falling like pools of sunlight do –
Across a sombre, murmuring plain;
I did not follow the curving road
But made the turn through an unnamed gate
And followed a dawn of choice – into the chosen way.

A salute to Trisha, Howard, Jo, Mary, Peter, Charlie, Geoffrey, Virginia, Imants and Jennifer – all the protagonists around that table.

# Towards another summer

There is a newborn calf dead by the yards
Its tongue taken at first light by a fox
A life swiped for a tongue, what an exchange –
Need is swift and ruthless in nature.

In days then weeks which pass while
September wind sways in the creaking conifers
The fallen shape is stripped down to sketched white bones –
Life, like the maggots, feeds fervently from death to survive;
And a year unravels its mosaics of circling patterns

New light and old darkness renewing
And retreating, erasing and replacing a brace of seasons
Stepping forward and then back –until it's spring again
And as if nothing had happened –

And we see a crow perched for a wing-beating moment

On the coiled white ribs of last spring's death –
The calf's head pristine, cushioned by daisies
And a mound of clover; ants crawling through the eye sockets
Have carried away a hundred times their number and strength

And the mother has given birth to another calf
That bleats and butts and punishes up under her udder
Bellowing before it finally gets a grip on the teats
Tugs down and sucks for its right to life, under skies shifting

Constantly onwards, sailing toward more lofty cathedrals of light –
And the single death of last spring is taken for granted
Blurred in a surge of luscious green pasture
And pendulums of yellow buttercups
While slants of summer fall, golden blessings across the emigration of grasses.

# A human weathervane

I've been on a horse
For days, head down into this august wind
A human weathervane, cantering across dark fields.
August is always the dying month
They say in the wind-strewn hills hereabouts.

The cows are lying down
Ready to calve, the foxes wait up
Crouched close, for the prized calf's tongue
Hanging loose, drooling for its mother's milk.

For the fox, an easy paté gained with one lunge…
I ride up and down the forest line
Scaring fox's eyes away
Saving tongues and mothers ready to lactate

But some will not escape – despite this
A job as well done, I suppose
As any might be at four o'clock in the morning.
The tongues, apart from those in moribund dreams

May appear later, in some candlelit place
Seasoned and salubriously served
On a glowing silver platter
With herb mustard or bechamel.
But that is a different matter

Another chapter, beyond the birthing of a calf.

# Indifferent skies

A farmer on his porch
Watching silence
And nothing happening
The paddocks of years of labour
The fences with no intentions left

The gates with no plans to close
The dark clouds came
Puffed with promise
But no consecration
Just a breeze, waking
A few creaks in timbers

You could walk about
The house paddock, the yards
Boots sunk in expensive dust
Instead you'll creak out of your seat
And go and make another tea.

The house echoes now
Everyone's gone, floorboards
Groan back, memories' ghosts flicker
Coming and going, a
Hide and seek of fading whispers
Furniture stuck in timeless poses
Outside, standing over the entrance steps

He watches the crows
Circling overhead
Cawing, cawing, cawing – anyone there?
Hello? Hello? – Anyone there?
No one? –well on our way now, nobody there
Wings beating muffled wingbeats
Across rusted galvanised iron, then

Silence –a long, trailing flight away
No clouds to get in the way
Then further on, a drifting composite of dots
Fading suddenly like a cry
Swiped, kidnapped by the wind.

He remembered once
In a time as dark as this
He had heard lightning
And looked at the sky
And he had cried, really happy
So very happy, as heavy drops
Splattered down over his drawn face
And the tumult drove mist
Rolling languidly all around the place –
He walked through the soaking mist
Like a man with a gift of a second life.

The tears then were not the same
They were really sweet, not just wet
They trickled cool and tingling
Down cheeks into his mouth
The tears now
Are wasted and spent
Alien and vagrant, sparse like
The silence – of an empty, indifferent, sky.

# A wounded splendour

A tree is shedding leaves of minutes and moments
The leaves of faded golden hours
The drifting days, swirling weeks and years
The leaves of all the harvests
The flocking of endings, scattering
Into a silent theme, each dry, dry
Leaf a blossom of life, finally letting go

A page, another, floating away
A drifting requiem
Of different times and places –
Each leaf a footnote, and a comma
To time spent well or regrettably unwell
Life undressing, undressed ephemeral flesh
Drifts in coils, drifting into the spiritual

A wisp, a stream, of fragments of time
A cloud of memories' shadows dispersing
Into another light, unburdened as a vanishing life
The minutes and moments circle, time unfurls
You hear a whisper, a murmur
Floating to childhood, you remember a cry, a simple joy
Of innocence; a dream that flared, which could not, would not last –

The dream is swirling, floating onwards
Scattering, dancing into pinpricks of light
Leaving branches nakedly bereft behind –
Leaving more of the sky
Leaving more of the moon
Leaving a vanished season
And a distant mood of motionless stars

Leaving a long day's moment of the past.
The leaves of hours swirl about
More now, billowing and flowing out
The clouds of time, unwritten
Are drifting slowly over
Dipping and rising, blossoms of life
Gliding into different, unknown light.

# Driving to cicadas

The cicadas' song rises
As I drive through a curve around a corner
As I change gears, throttling down the years –

The remembered chant lifts, flows
Along like a rhythmic hymn
A chorus of a million small voices

Congregating up there – a continuous song
The humming dirge merges
With my weaving, zigzagging journey –
The sky is mine now they seem to sing.

Do they seek to claim time
Make it stop, possessed
by passion and song
do they seek to keep time, like a lover, enchanted?

Car, cicadas and memory
Becoming one shining whirring thing
As we hurl ahead, the car
Flanks gleaming light and passing, reflected trunks of forest –

One same song I hear clearly now, on another summer day
As I turn the wheel again, the same curve, the same corner
Blurring – Pulling me inwards, a melodious drift
flows across a surfing chorus – the thrumming of my years –
for moments again my life stops, held by the cicadas song.

## Pagan moon

The moon spends
Some of the past it hoarded
Memory tonight
Is slowly unfolding
A fan-shaped story.

You share a burden
Of remembering
A golden stream
Of moments and people
Enough to populate this park, enough
Of those statues of those gods that talked things over
Before strict divinities, before

Common sense prevailed, answers you want
Are not possible, these gods have been
Alone, idle, on pedestals much too long, the moon lends golden light
In memory of them, how much time has it been
Since they have answered the prayers of anyone.

A small, misplaced mortal
You sit under heroic company
Becoming a little younger
Becoming a little pagan
Mesmerised by the moon
And the shadows of the illustrious.
You cannot turn another page
Of thoughts, in this silence

This golden hoard of silence
The sensible, fearful self might
Want to walk away from –
Walk away from the menace of magic?
Hurrying now, back across the park again
Taking the track, a shortcut towards home
Quickly before, before it happens –
Oh no –your slowly stiffening bewitchment?

You know your moonlit street
Real, functional, planned and cautious, wants you back
The opened window there will be watching
Flickering, slanting signals, impatient for your return
But your ear has succumbed to the silence

Again you pause along the track
And turn around, now
You are deaf enough to hear
It – now, going back the years
The sound no child fears;
Thrilling to bewitchment
When the moon speaks out
Softly so, in her beams of molten silence.

# Cascade

'I remember gestures, descents of giving me water.' – Gabriella Mistral

The waterfall ricochets
Splintered and white
You drink the idea; cascade
A leap and wild chance swirling away

Everything falls –
Hope is the great defier of height
You keep your mouth right to the chalice

Life the long drink
Air and mist the elixir
Falling in needles and threads without, within

And the frothy idea from a sip, then a gulp
Lasted three days, hope
Rose like a spiralling swallow

With a long, trailing link of water
And flew far away, a dot, a message
Hope emigrating slowly into brightness.

The valley is not the same
Any more; serene, eternal as always
And the waterfall falls into its song as it did before
Eloquence, grace and silence descending

But the idea has faded
Gone into mist and cloud now
It's as if the thread

From the bird's beak
Was tugging away
A trail of words
Then it broke, perfectly unsaid.

# Return to the silence

It seems as if nothing
Is happening
Except a room
Is composed, waiting
Sternly, perturbed, for its occupant.

Could you have been here before?
Is it possible that chair was once yours?
Light falling on the wall
Is in some familiar way, curiously faded.
Time is not quite the same any more

Just inside or outside either
Through that half-open window
Or that hallway door – all is expectant
The room with a single chair
Is remembering

And reaffirms it will remain the same.

Shall you go into the room?
Or respectfully stand back?
Instead your memory, curious
Enters softly – and sits
Comfortably again in the chair
Becoming part of that light and time then

Becoming a part of that life again; once
Lived recklessly, without fear or doubt
About consequence
A time and a way to live
That suddenly fell into a slant
Ending unplanned, with no one
To tell, a stillness
With one silhouette
Witness on a faded wall.

# Embers to ashes

Tongues of flame
Flicker in the quiet
Back and forth
A contented, dancing chorus
A tapestry of autumn
Is silence intrigued with itself?
A phone blinking, another message unanswered
Stillness a presence, expectant in the house.

Silence has settled as secretly as dust
Are you finally getting tired of life?
The exhausting thoughts of dying –
A return to the unknown dimensions of the earth?
Inborn persistence won't let you sidestep
This question, you explore and explore
Turning the slow pages of more thoughts

But nothing you know will illuminate here
The light doesn't reach the dark, quizzical corners
Of a room, or corridors of a taciturn home. Stars on high
Are there wherever, but scattered
Into their own schemes, into their own orders
Light has come and gone in distant windows
Outpaced by dark across the fields, leaving shadows
Of silence in leaf-shorn vineyards and olive groves.

Who says darkness does not answer? –
And does death have a gender?
Does it come as a man or a woman? Is death a marriage
Or a divorce? No one ever taught you
About this inconvenience, Mario this morning
Said living with death is no simple matter
They say in the village, life is death
And death is life – death is part

Of an unsung harmony – poor Mario
Who lost his mother the other night
Consoles himself again in the stables below
Talking alone to his favourite cow –
I said to him, death has stood aside for life
For a long time, death wants to resume its place
In the treacherous equation, the flames

For a moment blaze, like something alive
While embers weep ash into an ending
Yet life will fight back
Wild and angry, watching your ragged
Breathing, your thoughts bleeding
Into the disbelief of dawn.

## Still, not yet forever

The clouds wait
As if in a painting
The sun has risen, paused
Behind a veil of whiteness.

Sky and wide, arching dome of silence –
The painting waits to begin
A mist of shadow low down
Covers the land, suspended

For a signal, is this the first or last moment?
Or is it memory waylaid
Or about to turn now, going back
To where it thought it was before?

Or is this in the subconscious?
An image or a prophecy of an ending
Autumn, shadows, a litter of loss –
Shadows reaching for

Dark freedoms –the horizon dreaming
Of once upon a time;
Of early light, just for one moment
Still, not yet forever.

# Dust and time

You stare into boredom
Like an art form
A window
On monotony.

This is not like gazing at lint
Or dust descending
In a space of minutes
In air made golden –
That is focus.

This is becoming utterly
Insignificant, watching nothing much
Happen – it is as if the dust
Actually watched you –the lint
Descended to get a better
Look at your paralysis.

These tiny specks
Will continue to descend
After the human they examined
Is spent and buried – after you are cleared
From the shelf;

'Remember me,' you whisper
But the dust does not listen.

# What light can do

Light does not change in the exile
Of your being; the island turning, journeying inside
You need to frequent at strange times
Dreaming awake or fast asleep…

The foreign lands you leave
Alive, real, to friends who would never return to here –
Places you have been and still nurture
In a decades-long love affair, when your eyes

Delighted in marvels of architecture
And stalked days of other centuries
Searching exitedly through ancient streets
And the essence of medieval art rested, a feather on your shoulder, the skies

Of Etruscan empires and tapestries of the renaissance; banners
Of blue and white skies, heraldic, played out beside and inside your head.
Today in the second half of your life
The vaporous scaffolding of southern skies

Tempts you to explore, now differently, explosions
Of spokes of sunsets, deeper crimsons, ochres
To consider rather than fresco-faded reds…
Balancing, the bouncing clumps of dancing eucalyptus

Rather than contemplate the sombre cypresses, the pilgrim trees
Paused like monks in smouldering green cloaks.
You know what light can do; moving with the dawn of a Tuscan city
You have felt the shivering thrill of watching people

Wake and start to move about in streets of well-trodden history
Like protagonists of a depicted, earlier age; moving awake in brown antiquity
With the bells ringing, tolling a layered melodious tongue
While you held yours – a language half-formed under your breath

Until you learnt to pronounce those round, luscious vowels
And caught the eye of a Florentine madonna who became your own renaissance.
Today, as you take your long walk along the curving reach of sand
And look well beyond the exuberance of surf, where headlands

Head to head, nudge one another in cantering endings
Toward the curves of the pacific sea; you can still haul those fragments
Of temples back and whim those Tuscan towers
To sink with your southern sunset
Its fire spreading a tapestry of hills of vineyards and towers
Over ongoing swells of Southern Pacific waves
Long trails of sparkling light drifting
Underneath a new world's clouds and skies
As blue and white as those porcelain madonnas

Fixed along streets above studded doors of Florence.
What light can do and does well and will serve you
If you have a world-jumbled eye and want to make
Two places float inside your vision
With a shaft of golden light between two worlds…

This afternoon, about to be evening, you stroll
Along under lengthened spears of a laggard sun
The new moon rises and the rustling wind comes
Dusk spreads with daylight softening, floating and dispersing –

Yet days of Italy and her clamorous streets
Her sing-song language, her aged and young eager
Faces, her banners, her bells, her chimed farewells
Still echo, still float in these southern waves, crashing endlessly.

# Green silence

The silence
Of this green Tuscan hillside
Is perfect, serene
You hear your breath
Measuring it

The path taken
By the cypresses
Two files climbing together
As if they were always there
Forever paired

In the journey to the crest.
The peace, the light, the stillness
Seems eternal, even
Now with your eyes closed
The cypresses persist
Twinned, elliptical, symbols of hope.

# Land's dialectics

A way of speaking terrain
That line rolling between
Field and forest
Invisible and precise
Reveals two undulating greens
One etched across with sunlight
The other, embroiled
Leaves of dark and glancing light

The movement of boughs
In the wind, arms
Labouring, trying to climb
A flurrying plumage
Of plunging, leaping leaves doing
Whatever it wants
Intense greens churning, so much churning

A bit like the mind
Trying to rinse out dislike
For platitudes or convenient solutions.
Wind, cloud, storm, all weather
And all turbulence
Please save me
From cosy miracles –

Grass criss-crossing; alert
Green all ears, or just on the run?
Lulls of light waft and wave
Through calmer blue afternoons;
A distant farmer's lonely dog

Now barking loud and long enough
To wake up Munch from
His reverberating dream – and I hear – 'the scream' –
Nature and man hopefully
Could be shaped into one good resolution
Yet no such thing exists, no way, no way
Everywhere unlived and rarely explained –
The fear of nature and the need
To govern her, cruelly, rules
Endures, like a damned marriage.

Walking underneath branches
Of bird-talk, bowed, adorned
With chattering sounds like a harem of warbling's –
But no matter how much
You have come to love, to adore them –
Their stoic, dozing, stalwart greens –
You won't let yourself fall sleep
Or dally at all in the woods today or

Ever again, but skirt around them

Like a great American poet Robert Frost, did
At dusk once – heading
On from memories
Leaving beautiful trees
To their immense mystery
Further and further behind –
Trees and greenness
To brood singularly – shadows tethered
Seeming to be listening

Lengthening into memory
But finally to be left there
Abandoned, magnificent, intact.

# Unlit window

Meet me where
We watched the crabs
Dancing on the moonlit sand
And I walked behind watching your footprints
Remain for seconds, erased by golden waves

Kisses in the deeper shadow
Of a roman pine, now lingering in a moment's mind-storm
Your naked breasts breathtaking
A shock offering
Leaning on a rock while we watched
The crabs dance; real, real, not stuff of dreams
The fan-shaped foam whispering

Chasing so many dancers up the glistening sand –
Today I flinch remembering
The promises we so passionately made
Forgotten in the following, few days
Youth and short memory allowed
You and me to be easily elsewhere and tonight
Infected by a full moon, you now return
Gliding into the past, into the gull-echoing sepia.

Sunshine returns with a cloudless day, left alone
In the unlit island of your room, half-light
Enhances your daydreaming mood
And as far as you know you are the one creature
That still moves through that frozen sepia, you reincarnate
Those moments, faces, lisped words, laughter
Of those that have mostly vanished, as the immense
Shadows of the past become tiny, dissolving

Into the static of nothingness; dust and ashes
Of what happened, a last slow spiral of smoke in time –
Night and its ending in dawn, the first low-lying light
An unfolding white page
For a new day, darkness retreating
Into farthest corners, plundered again by dawn
Harvester once more of the hidden, a litter of shapes and things
Neglected throughout a night's blindness.

Mid-morning; the swallows return, bringing bark fibres
Threads, anything to finish their nests, hope borne
In circling and swooping swirls
The future, a precarious future, held in their beaks.
Nothing ends; you have watched them
For years, returning to repair last spring's nests
Nothing ends; nothing remembered ends
A testament there to tell, a moment there to share
In the light remembered again of an autumn afternoon.
The second day has ended;
Dusk creeps, begins the rebirth of shadows
Stars return, flung out celestial embers
Miles-high messengers already dying or dead
Sing their song of curvature beyond
Millions of light years; the trees' bare boughs
Underline the sense of – is nothing left?
However the silence is weightless
With the quietness no sense of harm
You watch and listen to the meticulous
Language of darkness; perhaps nature listens
And also wants to know what you are made of –
You are a well known secret; a human being

With probably too many codes to unravel
The unlit window is your outpost
You remember many things as you watch and listen;
Children absent, inhabiting other worlds
Hopefully undamaged through your own or others' ignorance –
The fallen, broken branch still blossoms in June
But the blooms cannot carry the broken arm back up to the tree –
Our children drift, blossoms once, now flowers
Petals blowing astray in the wind; alone
We remember the first word, the first good step
Joyously taken in distant rooms, then farewells
As they carry their hope and purpose, their youth
Into the glinting promise of a distant future –

The window stutters suddenly with a gust of wind
You shiver with recollections –
Oh to return across the sand, stand before the golden serenade
Of the rocking, swaying sea, oh mother moon take me
To where the gentle waves crash
Take me back to the golden sands
Where the crabs so nimbly, dance, and
Let's begin that kiss again in the shadows
A flowering that cast the seed of everything.

# The old place

Time runs away in stars
Across the windshield glass
Racing against the dark

Streaming on past
As quick as it comes, the wind
Will smooth away

The random lashings of rain –
The grass curves goodbye in the wake behind.

As you step out of the car
Memory cloaks you in a blur
Night birds you remember, some announcing your return.

The moon hesitates, balks to offer one mellow word
While steps you make toward the porch
Seem to be foretold, you walk in an airless

World where even your own breathing
Seems remote, two steps and then a stumble, after
Floating over the boards, the door, it's still unlocked…

The polished planks of the corridor
Creak along down toward a steady glow, you know
Black labrador dogs, illuminated, silvered by the fire

Are asleep just out of sight; around
The flickering corner, winged armchairs
And a lumpy Victorian couch, all wait for sure

With a famous painting of the same room
Brushstrokes slowed by tongues of a glowing lamp
The mantelpiece clock will tell the same time

Above the hovering specks of fire –
Suddenly deep bongs of the hall clock – long ticking
Tocking out of the frame of the mirror that gilded your parents' faces

Striking just before you turn…you turn the corridor –
Corridor to confront – confront an empty room again…
Hushed with the smell of must; ashes stirring
Dead embers glow – dead smoke
Coiled forever in a faded fireplace.

# Her coiled blue curves

He had loved the river from early days
And thought she had been misplaced
In the order of things; unsung, unpraised
Remaining unheard of all those years

With her sleek blues and her skipping silvers
Her way of curving under the gums
And swinging wider afterwards into the light
She glowed through, onward, then past borders, fencelines
Of the land he had luckily inherited –

Like an unearthed waterfall, borrowing as much of the greens
Or blues as she needed – gathering and losing
Retaining and releasing
And he liked the way birds
Flew, gliding up and down her course
Using her waters like a beacon, her shining continuing
To amplify their cries – sent flying onward to feathered kin

Hidden in the plumage of trees – or surprised, stalking the grassy water's edge.
The river remained in his mind; a living leap
An arabesque, a swish of living silver
When he journeyed through the world – and he saw her often again
One night in the Seine's undulating reflections – and as a twist of brightness

In the reddening sky above the Thames sluggish greys and blues –
He saw her in amongst the buildings floating in Manhattan waters
Rolling through the wavering shapes, the wobbling geometry –
He saw her in the Tiber; that seam
Of quicksilver triggering through the slow greens

While pausing and watching under the parasol pines –
In Piazza Navona he sipped his coffee
Missing her now – in front of Bernini's rusting travertine rivers
Sipping some wine
Thinking about her supple greenness – finally at the end of the long year
He returned, counting hours clicking southward over dusty bitumen

And running down through the long recalled paddock
He reached the unexpecting
River bank and squatting there beside her again, he dared to mention
All those rivers he had seen – but made little of it –
And allowed her to flow about his
Offered hand, dipping carefully into her faithfulness, like the feelings

When a favourite cat brushed him, coiling its tail around his legs.
It was good to be back; to continue the usual whispered talks of before –
She was his well-hoarded mistress, there was no doubt of this
And her beauty was best kept where it was, where now

She flowed on her own, under dusk or midday or dawn skies –
For him, her protector and no one else.

# The rock pool

Crouched down in the grass
You loved the way
The wind blew past
Too high to find you.

Or down by your favourite pool
In the creek where you waited –
Getting later for dinner, under
The arched branch of a reddening sky

The tadpoles forever, forever quivering –
Trembling to one place – until your father's urgent cry
Calling for you to hurry and come
And eat your dinner with mum

And him – facing the panes of the kitchen window
While you forked down steak, watching the way
The gum trees would shake in the wind, fascinated
By the way the crisp, swishing leaves

Tossed clumps of silver, back and forward again…
The keening cry of the crows, forging
Through red realms of sky, streaks of veering clouds
Left in long thumbstrokes; the calm following the vanished wind.

Today you have grown but the feathered redness
Of a sunset is still clear evidence
Of those times, and you can still sense
Your old self back there; like a leaf or a curved blade of grass

Lying, tumbled into wilderness – but the witnesses
Of your childhood life; of your treks to the creek and back
Have gone, skies of swallows drifted to somewhere else…
The proof of them continues to weather

In paired names, lichened into stone and their images
Sometimes seen in the vast quiet of clouds
Or floating half-written in the wind, speared by cries of crows
And just over the rise, a congress of clouds
Still speaking memory, drifting higher into Clyde mountains.

# Magic and sunshine

The moon with her bruised cheeks
And bone-white brow, cannot
Muster up any more emotions.
She has witnessed it all
Her slowed golden light
Is all she has left from before –

Her gilding is clinging to things
Pauses where it can get no further.
It's us who will have to shine
Devise inspiration, find
Within – our own gliding moonlight.
The cypresses reaching for the night-sky
Have grown into plumes of black silence –

They are not going to save us
Poised on their tips
Neither the moon will –
Once suspended so, was thought to be magic –
Nothing will save us, for we are only children
We have no sense of consequence

We do not know what we have and do not have
We can't read the signs, now we only have
What might be called common sense –
We know the moon balanced; a golden
Ball on the tip of a tree, is an illusion –
We have lost the gift of being charmed or thrilled

So we do not see the golden moonlight bird
Swoop low down to earth and disperse
In a glowing aura – we once knew the golden dust
On our arms and shoulders was proof;
The moon, the stars sensed who we were
Now the stars and the moon dissolve

In a languorous, logical, milky fog –
The moon is tired of this
And stops pretending
To charm its way through
Conspiracies of coiled mist
She knows the game is shortly over
Dawn is just there, over, below the curve
So much gold has now been stolen by cumulus

And we, tucked up, like all good children were then
Kept one eye cocked for the good fairy
Coming soon to save us – until eyelids dropped
And the dream, to come, came tip toeing
Past and through those shadows watching over us –
Darkness watching how our eyelids closed
And then in our childlike minds
Across the plains of tides –
Golden sunshine arrived and began to flow.

# The woman walks

Hooded in her thoughts
The woman walks
As a woman would
Determining how much

Love has cost, how much
Love has given, how much
Love has gone, how much
Love is useless now –

The woman walks
Knowing how much
She, alone, must decide
The journey of her days

The nature of being alone.
Somewhere she knows
He will also walk, for how long, alone
She could not hope to know

Nor how long he would need
To forget – a woman walking somewhere
On her own; a woman hooded in her thoughts –
Time flowing already, over what was surely gone.

# Bunyah

For Les Murray

Gold waistcoated, gliding
Guru of the sky, sun
The darkness dispeller –
Moon pensive with
A penchant for gilding –
A long distance smile
From her bruised-bone-yellow head.

Here the trees rest
Leaves sleep, spent
Silence hovers in suspended realms of silence
Moonlight gilds time, swirls
In coils of left over wire
Gates wear moonlit braces.

What to do with this complicit existence
Fungus and sinuous roots unseen
Trees are touching underneath
In a midnight of earth
Existence goes on –
The river is surrendering, swishing
Her flowing silver arabesques.

Pasture gossips in bunches
Language pauses at the borders
Of things, in awe of illiterate magic
Night with its dawdling pools of light
Martians are probably summarising –
Drowsing iron roofs converse
With sidelong glints
Moment by moment

Things are measured by different light
Light ticked over by unseen time
The mind wandering up and down
Avenues of thought, not knowing much
Nobody about – impatient for a sign
Some glowing thing – to caress and touch.

## Ashes of silence

The heart's ash
Those flecks of fire
Swirl and rise
Ripened in silence.
Ghosts of beauties
Clothed in spring leaves
Move through me

The blossoms
Held on, but could not remain
The glowing fruit faded
My palms clasped hope
For the last hopeless hymn;
The bees' swarming chorus;


Through honey-slow slants of light –
A warning of imminent hibernation
Humming prophesies of autumn to come.
Leaves sweep, sighing, whispering high and low, like thoughts
Falling over a field, shaking free of memories
They will scatter, journeying, onward
Wasted pilgrims lost in the sinuous, woven grass

But come to rest and please, now, memory stop
And forgive and learn to forget
Whatever the cruel darlings said
Now those fickle smiles are frozen
Now those dazzling promises slowed
Into a groaning monotone – yet
My palm still brushes the neck
The shoulder, the thigh, some other
Cheek of mellowed brightness

Your face up there, floats again in a jigsaw
Of naked branches, your beauty disdained
To dismantle me, all too easy, it preferred
Terror to beguiling tenderness
It preferred a fool
Who by habit, had to remember –
A fool who touches you now
Fingertips blackened
Where happiness
Had lingered.

# Heaney's wind

Stopped by the cliff edge
Standing close by the rocking car –
Torrents of wind flowing and you catch
Still holding the freezing doorhandle –
A sudden blow of comfort…

You are reminded of Heaney
His slow stoic lines of verse
Driving those four muddy wheels further
Hunched in his cosy car island
Slowly following the cliff's edge in County Clare.

His thoughts bucketing sideways
His heart buffeted suddenly upward
Like a kite twisting and turning in the sky –
And you stand away from the shaking vehicle
Freed of the cold, chrome grip

Watching the glow of a sunset, a galleon in flames sinking
Your thoughts tugged closer to the cliff…

Standing away from the shuddering province of your car
Facing the light's rush, while it floods into every crevice –
Even your saddest secrets…sluggish in the leaps of light
And you suddenly grab for your hat, flown

Into the streams of light and emotion…
A favourite old cap, gone with a gasp
Wrenched from somewhere in your guts, your wings
Of curses floating up too fast –
Flying beyond your stretched, transparent hands.

# Once a Swedish poet

In memory of Harry Martinson, 1904–78

If you step outside the cabin door into the chill of the morning
And you look about where you knew he went on his walk –
And following the trail of a moose or the paired pricks of a hawk or raven
You might still see a footprint of his, surviving the days already gone…
And then go to the mantled cairn of stones on the crest
Where he paused in summer
To watch the white birds swing and glide over the furrows of ploughed land
As he stood knee-deep in grass blown furious by the wind
His cap in his hand and his hair threading the flow of air.

However, it is probable you will not find him at first
Even if you peer further into the half-dark forest…
You may turn in a circle with your eyes upturned to the sky
And also be no wiser, but if you crouch and keep silent he might return to you
In a sigh of wind or in a leaf that may tumble onto your shoulders or your head –
For the poet is just as present as the cool air
Now hovering over blue ice and snow
And look and you will see how some of him falls in the dry white powder
Drifting from the wind-ruffled branches of conifers as they swing and sway –

And to the west on a clearer day some of him drifts high above
The depthless blue aura of the mountains
And down here nearer, a part of him will always be there, hovering
Over the landscape of marching forests
And floating like a page blown every way
Over dips and rises of the sun-yellowed plains –
And his words, spilling, now streaming closer
Are shadowing pure white ground
Like the seeker birds swooping over the rose-tinged snowdrifts.

# The man without leaves

The beech tree reaches high
Into the fields of grey winter sky
Bare tips stretch toward the silence of clouds –
Throwing a bouquet of white branches

A fractured fresco up against accumulating sky.

White filaments flaring like
Remembered fireworks, like an idea
Photographed, a negative, frozen in the mind…
Below the tree is the same naked man again, standing there

Head thrown back looking up a trunk rising to light

His outstretched arms tremble affinity with criss-crossing tendrils
The drifting gaps of blues and whites, fingers spread
In communion with the cold earth and winter sky –
The shaggy white dog panting beside him looks

At the man's fingers fluttering, and knows already
The man is thinking up a poem called 'man a tree alone in winter' –
And his bare arms swing wide, as he turns around and around
And the dog sees again the naked man has lost

Every single one of his leaves…
But remembers it would be normal for this time of the year
And the glazed marsh lying around the man and tree
Is simply a mirror surrounding a solitary being's heart…

The dog has watched, waiting for him to thaw all these years
And now he watches again as the man's arms rise
To brace and lift the burden of an unanswering white sky

To hold back a landscape of whiteness in the sky
Which will not resolve itself and will not roll or glide or thunder either –
Nothing will come to the earth now, nothing will be released in drops

Or flakes, or even hail, nothing given in warmth or raining comfort…

And spring watches everything, from an unthawing peak
Knows some of her tears, still frozen down there
Are stored in the heart of that man –
A man leaning, intent, into a cold wind – with no more leaves to spare.

# The friend who flew away

The budgerigar flew
And perched on the book
He was reading
And nibbled the tops
Of the pages he was turning.
One day a gust of wind blew the window open

The boy still grieves
The bird escaping
A green and yellow blur
Over the rooftops
Smaller and smaller
Fading further and further, then at last forever.

Maybe one morning
The boy dreamed
A miracle would occur
And on the upright book left wide open
The budgerigar was perched
And every chirp was a joyful chime

And the helpless voice of grief
Following the flight into silence
Echoing for years, was broken
And beyond the window, left wide open
The bright sky strummed again
And memory trembled, in a limpid, new light.

# A cliff of sky between the birds

'The gene we have in common allows us to speak and for them to sing' – Margaret Atwood

The last of evening light leans far off
Endless all the way east, white trunks
And reaching branches of gum trees
Bathe in this light's long high tide.

Closer, slower, Lombardy poplars move ahead
Like glittering, spectral fountains, migrating across
The stubble of paddocks, pausing and continuing
Up along the hillcrests and over the undulating ridges.

The book I put down blurs chapters
In the dusk breeze, thoughts flicker and flutter
But do not settle; winter has lost its bite
The days are getting longer and blue-sky banks

Higher every evening, rising against altering light.
A molten mass of coral cloud hovers, burns like
A refrain of a bulging concerto
And crows drift like notes against lingering fire.

In this hour you sit in one of your father's or maybe
Your mother's, interchangeable chairs
And sip your tepid tea and remember
On an earlier shadowed porch, how they ritually watched

The way the sunset and the ranked rows of forest trees
Played their game in fading light, all of this a subtle
Nuance of enjoyment, relished every evening – until the divorce –
Then the rules all changed and suddenly

All arrangements would never be the same.

My eleven-year-old mind saw them in another play –
As I imagined them like two huge ungainly birds, uncomfortable
Now with anyone's company, their unwieldy human wings grew suddenly
And they flew a short distance away; and they walked

Stiffly on the lawn keeping an eye on the porch
And settling on me, conversing obliquely in their bird language
Seeming ready to migrate, to take off into the day beyond
Before finally vanishing where I could not see far enough to follow.

Years later, grown enough to finally get out of a boarding school
I remembered how the crow was entering their voices –
The hoarse croaks edging further out towards the sky
And how their posture changed; how they hunched, tails down over

Their separate concerns; old certainties lost in awkwardness
You sensed how they seemed to be abandoning things
Burying the outer layers, shedding
Their feathers and claws, beaks pointing
To newer eclipses, leaving their feathered personae

Like something ruptured and flung aside, souls inside-out
In two rumpled piles on the boards; each left behind a curving flight.

# Wind with a different destination

Young once you trusted
In a secret destiny
But there was none to come
You were just crashing through
The boundaries of chance.

Blissfully unaware, untouched
Chance was your sole destiny
And everything else a happy accident –
Other feet and minds full of thoughts
Now walk those paths

Who have no memory
Of the moon, the light, the dark
You saw, they sort through
Different shades and names
With different faces

Shadows once tethered have shifted
They wait for the sway of different
Pendulums, today on the last hill
With the dusty whine of a dry carafe
The last, good red half – of – a – glass, left

You watch the wind whip
The sheets on the clothesline
Likewise the clouds, like sails
Tugged and torn across the ocean's horizon
Like destiny, like chance
Tossed in the dancing sibilance of surf and foam.

# Shadows of journeys

Standing up, he drifted in the dinghy
As if in a dream, drawn ahead by threads of islands
In the direction of another sky, another light of dawning.

Chortling sounds back under a bridge
River water churning eternally past
It's what brought him to this place

Escaping the past, escaping the fading faces –
Arriving, bumping up against
This pier, this landing, and then easing into the placid sea

A dream of water winding its way
From where the waterfall had roared
Then fell into silence, reborn as a curve of silence. The sea

Glimmers with a moonlit quietness
And his fingers twitch as he thinks
Of things he loves, weightless things

That will not budge, things

Of the heart grown so cumbersome
He nearly unbalances, stoops and stops
Bent forward in the gliding dinghy.
Love plucks tufts of memory now
Like a breeze in the grass and a lost summer guitar

Dark strings of passion tremble
With leaves somewhere
And the islands have since fallen behind –
Just ahead across the sea

Voices sing, praising creators and all mermaids and muses of water;

A sweetly poured out contralto
A gentle crescendo contrasting the sounds
Of the roar arched over into silence above a waterfall.

Will he be amazed, rubbing his eyes
To reddening, dozing islands, to scarlet undulations
Moving across another sea? Drifting into a different dawn, gliding

Towards a vast, unnamed emptiness ahead.

Will he wake to be in a place where
He can still remember vividly
The faces belonging to echoes of voices he knew?

So many faces in mislaid photographs
So many, where they will gather and share his fate
Every one in the gliding, urging dingy, shadows with voices
Shadows that hover and brush, mumbling beside
Fellow pilgrims, travellers who are fading just like him
Drifting in dreams over those shadows and softening light of memory.

# Absences

'Give me another life and I will be singing' – J. Brodsky

Stuck with the same old one
You only get the one, friend, the wise guys say
While chewing the same sour crust
A life forgetting is endless time –
How short the moment
Of love was, to kick-start it or to suddenly end it –
Passion kindling, licking lovingly and gone like a thief
Or a flame's shadow across the floor
Crossing the threshold, thrown
Out the door, before you see one flicker more.

Yet the hills of your arms
Your thighs, your breasts
Of full, lush milk – still persist –
In parted shadows fallen from thoughts
Your face plays hide and seek – those
Eyes following you, as you strive uphill

Strive up the heights to forget
While now the path shifts ahead
Slides narrowly and widely like a snake escapes.
Oh you are tired, oh you ache, ache
Memory is a long rope
It teases, it curls and it tugs
It winds back around you
Tosses coils through a tumult of thoughts.

Into this tunnel of time narrowing ahead
Light retreats and memory stubbornly follows in step
Dips in and out of time, memory
Savours things, is utterly ashamed or revels in things –
Whereas the moment comes and goes, a dusk
Does not divulge, promises nothing

Nothing astonishing; a blur vanishing like a hawk
Into a dawn wind – no use to plead
With something that's set on going
See how love has seeped out, breathless now
With a few last wing beats, no good looking any more
For its shadow, happy, melancholy or forlorn
Maybe some fallen feathers

Is all you're going to get
Curled, scorched, scattered on the floor.
What to do, what to do? Walking
Under a stream of emigrating birds
The flock that swayed rose and fell to a conductor's baton once
Now a darkening, steady mournful tumult
What to do, what to do? Your shadowed curves

Are now in the darkest wind, dreams dispersed in leaves
Drift in a litter billowing behind, you tire of being
A man, you tire of all your outlasting plans –
Is there no other way to be?
You are tired of love's needs, of memory, a life of memory
That swoops with its wings low over your head

Your shadow is still in the darkening wind –
Let us forget, yes – and step onward quickly
With no regret – we need
Something real there
Whole and malleable in our hands
In our trembling fingers, a last chance
At the darkening hour of the day

Ah yes – and to have a wake
A daylong, drunken wake
A staggering wake for the living –
Poor things, easily tricked
Adrift in and out of time
Inebriated with life, unable to die.

# Pebbles and memory

I'm not in the mood today
For clouds gambolling along
Chasing miles of a carefree sky
I am more concerned
It's coming to the end of the holiday

I was just getting used to –
This lithe suntanned world
And the same young one
Licking her gelato
Striding past in her rollicking way
Giving me a tasty smile, tossing her blonde mane

As she passes perilously close by my bar table
In her ridiculously skimpy bikini –
I'm also attracted to abandonment
Places usually open
Then closed, wearing a notice
A sort of obituary for a departed season
Interiors empty, shadows that seem frozen

But all of this absence
Could have waited a bit –
Summer was becoming a beautiful haze
And skies inscrutable, enveloping memories
Tatters of images, old thoughts
Now blown down empty end-of-summer streets
Like some vagrant, dreaming tumbleweed.

The journey is not over though

Through autumn's ochres
And rusting gold's, I will recall
It all, memory will plant old seeds for new
And I might even wear white linen again
Walking in the leaf-littered wind
Fingering tide-smoothed pebbles
And tossing recollections in my pockets, hearing
The far away crunch and roar
Toppling waves that recall, recall and recall
Rhythms and roars and brighter skies
That will never change, never go away
As I sip my cold white wine on a winter's porch.

# The Kiss

Her jumper tight-fitting
She twists to reach round and kiss him
Hugging, rocking as the carriage turns
Fingers caressing through the train's curving onward
And lips curl, engaged again as the train straightens
Jolting away into a tunnel now, echoes
In the dark – we recall early hollywood screens
Black and white shuddering moments –where the kiss

Can continue, soundless, untroubled, unseen.
Our lips are sensing memories again
As the clicks run crisper now
And the dark pulls its hardest and

We hear our heartbeats threading time and distance
Breathless while passing through thuds of darkness
And as the light rushes towards us
We glance again as they begin to kiss, another

Hug comes roaring into life – at the end

Of the echoing tunnel
the view widening
Light sweeping through
The kiss in memory luminous, eternal.

# Beach boy

He haunts the pool
Of his youth
Where the reflection did not lie

Now he sits on a rock
And peers across into the sky…
A much kinder distance.

The dovetailed music of birds
And the capricious curling
Of clouds, amuses him now

Where once he counted his ribs
Fingering earnestly, over and over
Peering into the pool; into his

Golden, floating face.
He knows now that beauty
Is an idea, tricked into being

By its stricken beholder. Oh how
It was simpler then
When a face was enough…

Without time
And truth, finally
Coming to dismantle it.

# A shadow's discourse

Shadows will murmur back
If you sit long enough
And watch them, as if
They know all about
Where you've been
And what you've seen.

See how they explore the floor
Inching ahead, to eventually enter
The wall, slipping under the skirting board –
Is there another world of light in there? –
Passing through to the other side of the wall?

The wall of nothing and then here-no-more – and
Again reborn, they may return, perhaps
As the offspring or facsimile, of that vanished shadow – now today
Until midday comes I usually have one constant shadow
For company, then gone, straying for a short while
At noon – but mine for the mornings
And afternoons, part of my slanting, advancing world –

Inevitably at twelve o'clock high it vanishes
For at least an hour or so, to go to wherever its peers
Disappear for lunch, uncertain, unhappy perhaps
About the doors opening and closing
Making shapes and space shrink, constrained to clinging
For a shadow's life, squeezed tight against one wall.

In the monotony of the office
They fall with scrutiny across
Submissions, passing over some pages quickly
Or lingering over those left open
With unresolved arguments; those forgotten
Old requests for promotion – or a little extra pay.
They will have followed the applicant's walk

Loyally to the chief executive's office
And matched those dejected steps back again
Clearly the promotion would never come true –
The moment for a new suit of clothes – was threadless years away –
The shadow lingers, darkly, now on pages
Of coffee stained notes from meetings, clearly

Too many meetings and too much scribbled ambiguity –
But most of all the shadow grows
Where dust knows well how to hide in light.
Shadows know nearly as much as dust does
About how long time waits – on that sill
Or in that unlit, gloomy corner
Or along that skirting board – a newly surfaced

Shadow does not reveal what might be in waiting
Or what, in a pause in a moment across the floor, it may
Be contemplating; an habitué of shifting time
And altered significances, a witness as well
In a domain of untraceable advances and retreats
Accomplice also in the realm of a mind, that often meanders over floors.

# The sight of lost time

You fall asleep
Into a tilting dimness
Reading the Gods had gone
Chapters and pages of lives
Swirled into dust in the closets of history.

Awake again, sleepless again, walking
Along over your old friend the leaf-padded pathway
Moving under the pin-oaks
Under a perplexed autumnal plumage

A bright star shines at the end
Of this parting river of leaves
Is this pulsing light the signal light of being?
Being that lives beyond its extinction?

You stop and stare up at time
Slowed in flight; this glowing panorama of silvered existence
While the river reminds you it is there
Still falling into the darkness, its roar

Descending through dark vastness
A cascade ringing onto unseen rocks
That will slowly fling light into the mist
When dawn arrives, when the roar

Is deafened by sunlight –but why walk
At this hour?– Dawns you've come and visited before
Why won't the night leave you alone, safe to rock and dream?
And then tug you awake with a few answers?

You suspect some of those answers may never come
Many things to remain always unanswered
The stars coming, curving up over the horizon
Are what has been – a timeless but expired light

Reminding you of simple remembrance –
The light of being that exists
Beyond its extinction –
But what will remain
Then, of us –
The light we uttered once
And left in transit?

# September in Renaissance Italy

How clever, autumn elevating
Death to beauty and celebration
Autumn the alchemist making gold
To glide with the flight of a leaf – clever
How the water is set alight, burning brightly
On a serene surface of an ornamental pond, clever
Embroiling the streams of golden light
In the branches of Roman pines; an orange horizon
Beyond; backdrop to the scrawling pilgrimage of trees.

The leaf following leaves is equally indifferent
An end is gilding its flight, as it floats across the wreckage of
the sun, down through the pedestals and busts
The pathways winding through the ancient gardens;
There is a nonchalance in such grace; death toying
With beauty, toying with time and timelessness.
Everywhere in autumn; along the Roman Tiber
Or the Tuscan Arno or over the bluish plains of Palladio country
Across the russet roofs, across smouldering towers of Venezia
Through the window of spiritual visions, religious retreats
High on snowcapped mountains in auburn, shadowed Umbria

Echoed in the leaves of flame curling and rising in fireplaces
In the stalwart stone farmhouses along the crests
The undulating, crimson-singed horizons of wintertime;
Dissolution is sketching out its last picture
Threads, patches left of summer; shedding
Its new nakedness, sounding its paling sonata
In the days advancing into the storms of darkness, or
The dark clouds raging north and south that do not seek an answer
But go swirling onwards into the northward veering valleys of winter.
Endless is the silence in the high song of winter-grey skies
The last orphaned leaf falling into a ditch, a gutter, a puddle of utter quiet
The last crevice of the forgotten, guarded by the stark trees
Their naked limbs cloaked in coldness and frozen blue and gold.

## Season aslant

All morning
A silent, painstaking, spider
The hand and pen, travelling
With memory, a shadow lengthening by its side
Flowing down line after line
Descending into stanzas, woven into webs

Of similes, echoes, maybe it's time to get up
From the desk, stretch a leg
Walk across a paddock
Look up at the heavens; refresh the mind.
Cattle now passing in an ambling
Anthology of four-legged Angus;
Mothers, calves, heifers and steers
Homing in on the river
Hoof-deep, a mingled, mutual drinking
Crowding reflections float under dimming, reddening skies.

Leaves falling, a season's grace
Doomed and steadily aslant, drifting
Into a heap, dispersed then in whispers of breezes
Briskly and impatiently tidying away the tinges of sadness.

And you now sense an urgency to go on
Striding along the crest
Fingering in your pocket, a favourite old coin
From the Italian days, sensing a sudden gust
Of poetry and wind and inclement weather
You distance yourself from the darkening forest
The darkening foliage, the darkening page –
Oh the curse of the human mind
Looking for trouble and finding it always –

And still keeping up the pace
Under a celestial weight of accumulations
Memories as usual, playing hide and seek
Skies on fire, a spectacle of disintegrating flame
Clouds like giant embers drifting, vanishing –
The cattle watch, turning big eyes your way
Always curious – and the spider dangles
Drifts on a thread, swings with tides of time and light.

The darkening day, the slopes turning
From green to black and you groan, more words
Jostle in your pocket, you begin again
To hear the rhythm, turning back
Along the cattle track, choosing linear time
Getting back to the sentinel veranda again
The expectant desk, pocketing more words
Netting words; some butterflies caught, to feed to the spider.

# Letter to a friend, in Florence

I envy you those shadows
When the city of stones
Turns to bronze and domes
Shine for mortal moments
Time fading over the hills of olives beyond.

What light can do, roaming at dawn
On humble surfaces, across
Cobblestones, rising on plastered walls
Of ornate facades, glinting, slipping
On iron grilles, molten for moments
A golden wash at dusk
Seeping out of winding streets –

And always, night and day
The river chuckles, resonates
Sweetly under the oldest bridge
Where Cellini, on his pedestal, keeps an eye
On how the clouds and sky, on a fine day

Misbehave; and the water rushes on
Underneath; anxious for more ancient history
And so on, travelling, flowing down to Rome.
I envy you your walk in the Boboli gardens
The order, the care; such green hope in artful geometry

The hedges that absorb
The sparkling music of light
Afternoons of parasol pines
Sailing on their optimistic journeys –
I envy you your café

From a favourite chair, you, witness
To the traffic of Florentines
Souls intently going about their days of moments
Passing with purpose back and forth, a moving foreground
To time and light-encrusted walls

Eyes occasionally lifted
To a dove or a pigeon suspended, wings lit
In a shaft of sunshine falling between palaces –
Or, someone, a stranger sitting anywhere

La bella Inglese, or, la bella Americana
Half focused on her coffee; thinking a thought
Or a memory for moments; the other unspoken half –
Of the beautiful watcher, watched by all
Meeting your foraging eye directly.

In the laneways of sunsets
Dawns and dusks
Under emigrating skies
I hear the footsteps again
Remembering where we once walked, talked together.

# Aphrodite?

So you leapt at last
Head out of a cresting wave
Light on your back
Like a dolphin
Curving down

Vanishing into the foam.
It was as if a veil had
Been drawn back
And cast away and from
A different light

I looked into your
World of raining light
Moments pouring when you
Flickered from girl to fish
Fish to girl, and later

When I remembered
You walking out from the sea, fingertips dripping
Hips glistening sparkles of light;
The roars shaking in droplets of water
Your kiss – a mix of grit, saliva and hisses.

# II

# Breathless in Exile

# Breathless in exile

Looking across the orderly ochres
Of Florence, a plateau of glowing terracotta
Domes dozing under crowns of circling doves
Marble facades dully, dutifully shining
The palace-lined alleys and avenues, crossed for years
Chasms of human traffic you knew by heart

Suddenly upstaged by a butterfly, its startling flutter
Such spasmodic breaths of flight trying to articulate
Something still unclear, a stutter of near-meanings
Or like poetry, a condensing of reality
Into both breadcrumbs and beauty.
Yes, poetry will survive history, if time resides in it.

The soul seeking something to hold
Finds words and the convulsive plunges of flight
Somehow echoes your sense of things
An ending, yes, yes, you know you will not return
To this congregation of golden-crusted
Medieval structures, rivers of stone
Winding past frowning, browed facades

But you will find words wherever you are
To set afloat her studded doors and arched windows.
In the thicket of lives, unknown, silent and vibrant –
Every one of us is an exile –yes, a momentary-seeking butterfly –
Today you have too many addresses, phone numbers
Which no longer answer, traces of those now fading away
Or launched forever into another heaven-sent flight.

Look how splashes of light fall from clouds
And play across the piazza onto chalk-white David
Over Giambologna's upward-spiralling, airborne humans
The glinting bristles of bobbing selfie-sticks.
Every man a friend of the piazza
Where the daytime drama of enduring sculpture goes on
Every man, a friend of the night, in shadow-draped streets
Walking home past smouldering lampposts, past arches

Through a brooding renaissance stage, walking after thoughts
Chased by footsteps following over rivers of old stone
Glowing where time resides, beginnings and endings shining
Like the flight of the butterfly, wingbeats of life
Remembered in sunlight, in flickering night-light
In the streets of Florence, where you spent time, breathless in exile.

# Ikos

The room on the other shore
Of the island, every window
Broken, was your borrowed home
For months of that unchanging summer.

You watched it glow to life
Every morning, during the day
Its lazing moods playing around the walls
With varying skies, until the long golden tide

Of the eternal evening; that time
Seems like the life of someone
You were still getting to know
Someone lean, agile, someone who lived for the sun

And loved a beautiful girl. The bed was narrow
An anxious fretful thing, but it did not matter
You slept rapt, entangled through time –
 Mornings swimming in the early light

Four legs dangling, torso and breasts
Bobbing, undulating together
Translucent water swinging you both
In its rocking Aegean – ancient wet warmth.

Rocks crouched to watch you;
Dark brothers at night, sleek blue sisters
At dawn; shoulders touching; with a blurring wind
To dry you, eternity spoke the wide sky

Silver emigrations spoke the midnight sea
The moon wrote golden testaments
Across upturned faces; all that in ruins
On the day of the leaves, streaming this way, that way

Like frightened mice; limbs of trees refusing everything
The sea leaping around you like so many dancing goblins
The sadness of the little boat, struggling forward
Towards another coast; another land obsessed with its own light;

Its wild charges of darkness, its rain wired
To foreshores blurred to greyness; summer
Torn into rags, tumbling behind, surfing in curves
Back towards the sisters, crouching, mourning

Now transforming to cloaked brothers; misfortune
Forgetting to close the broken windows, and
In the rocking, tormented boat
The resentful seething of the wind;

Memory still unforgiving in your fingers
Flexed, rubbed after the vanished smoke of a match.

# The poet in exile

In memory of Joseph Brodsky

1.

Buried on the island of Saint Michael
I picture you curled round
Your last memory of Saint Petersburg…

We knew you went to Venice every December
Better to nurture
Closeness to the lost city of your youth –

Its canals marbled the same way, traced with golden vapours of the sky
Its streets, mapped in your mind
Almost like the tidemarks of your adopted city Venice.

2.

I also was there, although I nurtured very little
Except a love for the carnival of arches outside –
The swimming choreography of swan white marble –

And my affection for a cloak, a cane
And a wide black Sicilian hat, I wore…

A composite of what I thought a poet
Would be inclined to wear in foggy Venice in the late autumn.

3.

Several times I passed you, not knowing
On the protesting staircase of the Pensione Academia

You looked like a clerk, in long service repose
You rose past me on the steps, balding –

Shapeless in your beige gabardine raincoat
One bulge, conspicuous, under your arm, hid a bottle

But a waft of nicotine is all we shared
Ascending and descending
And a generous wink from you once.

4.

Recognition of something you had sussed out perhaps
Maybe you approved of my Palermo hat.
A last ripe eyeful, a blink of irony
Before rising to your bare room above to write –
As I now know, your poem about the old Academia hotel.

5.

Armed with smokes and colourless vodka
Smuggled in under the beige gabardine

You rose to board the swaying crossing of the night –
From your rear cabin of the galleon, perched over the old canal –

While I descended to the swirling fog below
To walk amongst vagrant white Venetian tumbleweed, in company

With the blind tapping of my febrile mind…
Intent on the poetic, dressed as I thought
A poet best should, as he heads out, on a shadowy stroll through heaven.

# The swallows in Saint Peter's Square

The swallows refuse to assist
My eye's dismissal, tiptoeing in the air
Like those minnows, suspended in a stream

Of the moment, they hover then let go
And wheeling descend to slowly rise again, no flying monk
Could pull and allow his bells to topple

Roll over so eloquently, as these unconscious ballerinas of the air.

The priests that flow in pairs from St Peter's sway out across the square
And hardly lift their heads toward these tiny pendulums of flight
They grip their rosaries against the risk of an uncertain sky

And turn down the avenue in files; fluttering
Rags of darkness toward approaching night.

And as always I delay in this apricot-smudged square of Rome
And love to watch this autumnal show, the departure of the swallows
Signalled by their silent play, my eyes a little saddened

Want their farewell to be over quickly, my mind tucking away their salutations
But my heart tugs against this dismissal, hypnotised
By this continual swinging rhythm, a serenade to autumn

A flock of birds' last ballet in the changing rusts of light
Through a radiant gateway; time threaded for the traveller's eyes.

# Expatriate

Adrift, I think, is as good
A word as any
To describe this condition

After stepping from an aeroplane
To a train, then to a strange station
So many years ago, and not

Coming back, I circumnavigate
My original country, these homecoming days
Drifting in a dingy, so to speak, speaking

And dreaming in more
Than one tongue
Standing up unsteadily to see better

Where my old friends were, or
Might be still, amongst dots trickling along the shore –
The ones I knew in a life before

Whose quizzical gaze back into
My face today – defines little
More than the boy they once recalled

Who went away, vanished altogether on a certain day.
The streamers from railings to shore
Falling into the water

The thrust of the ship veering to point away
The faces framed, intersected by waving
Arms and hands, and what of that remains

That I left in a slow glide so far behind?
Enough to find a face again?
Enough to recognise a voice once more

Enough to step out of this little boat to say
Hey, hey, it's me, I'm back! I'm here again!
For a recurring moment in time

I remember moving behind that boy's face
Amazed, gazing, up at an architrave
A bust of a god or an ancient gable, the light serrated

By curved edges of roman tiles, a stranger
*lo straniero* – in a moment of gilded silence –
Looking, absorbing, through strange, ochre-shadowed streets

Hungry always for anything more to see
Standing at beginnings and endings;
Two parts of himself, his being, his heart

Paused in the slants of a different light
The balancing of memories
Swaying together, time's pendulum
Shifting momentum, from old to newly made.

# A chunk of heaven

'The city emerging felt like St Petersburg's extension
Into a better history.'
– J. Brodsky


A chunk of heaven dropped to earth
Infinity plunged to its knees in the sea
And here comes the blow-in – for goodness sake, me –
Abashed, lost in Italian, traipsing through
A dreamy melodrama of views, the sky courageous
Drifting on fire, the air drenched
In flavours of seaweed, the sky changing its mind
Dusk falling like a cloak over precipitous architecture
Echoes of footsteps, loss of direction
This is not your home, so where are your normal coordinates?

The water now a sliding mirror
For stars and the moonlit structures
Silhouetted line-ups move on, a mood, in measures of eternity
Sleeping domes, fluted chimneys dreaming
Smoke, sleepwalking towers survey
Rooftops, tidemarks of terracotta and
The Canal, unzipped, a curving striptease artist
Shedding turquoise and threads of gold, heading past
Peering palaces, arabesqueing out to sea.

You stop near a lamppost and watch
The long pendant of light
Slanting, wavering down through water
The city palaces have another life
Their darker twins mirroring
Golden facades above, swirling beside –
Frowning, stooping marble architraves advancing
Stern arches, cartwheeling, ranked intent towards water.

Ancient history drifts over blazing waters
Then the show goes out, late walkers
Striding alone, metronomes of steps in narrow alleys
High tide barely whispering, a slow languid
Lapping – you stop again under a Romeo and Juliet balcony
It's all the same, the old abandoned stage
Why do you return? The view will never be new
It is serenely the same, everything here
From monument to paving stone, waits
To be seen again. Is there a motive undiscovered –
Why frequent, why haunt this place? – You walk on

Into another piazza, who determines why Venice in winter
Is somehow better? – Unless you love deserted, breezy piazzas?
Ah – here is the pedestal with Niccoló Tommaseo
Perched up there on his pile of books
A good burger, our book-farter
'Cagalibri'– the locals of these parts
Have called him – A far cry from the lions
And noble, heraldic bronzes
Rising into view in or around St Mark's.
You find the few bare trees comforting
Looking like strayed pilgrims
Not quite sure why they are still in the piazza.

Under lamps attached to walls
The ongoing stones throw a pattern
A mortared hopscotch into the next moment
In a dark passage through an arch – no
It wasn't a ghost, just blinking green eyes of a cat
And the water-sliding sounds, everyway and back
As the solitary exploration progresses – under windows
Where the tinkling of knives, glasses, forks goes on
Families' robust, wine-fed, clatter-fed conversations
Other dimensions, tables of laughter, hovering above your head.

Keys in your hand, rising on the carpeted steps
To your room upstairs, you reflect on Brodsky
Who made this Pensione, in the Accademia, his winter pilgrimage
And wrote in those rooms overlooking the canal –
Such little risk or cost involved, you whisper, in using his old room
You might often dally with poetry, but you are a part-time exile
And you have not been forced to leave, ever, your country
Old friends or your lover or your father and mother, forever.

His ghost will not guide your hand or your pensive nib.
You look down over the vagrant mist
Wandering along the canal – will you ever know
Why you always come back? –
It's not just a lovely desolation
Marooned relics of abandoned beauty;
The moon is full and will not talk
The sombre towers and domes have other fates
To work with – the yellow light from lamps
Continues to scrutinise

The blue and green ooze
Of millennia – home is usually where the heart is
Or in this case, the pasta, or where wine-fed talk flows
But let's face it, poetry brought you here
And poetry has found a home here –
And Brodsky and others may be responsible
For all your hunger; this hunger here is another thing
Feelings amongst thoughts moving through murmurings
Of memories' lists, of notes of quotidian things – a dormant line
Of verse – is still looking for the right place
The right doorway – the right doorstep – where it might fall.

# Juggling Italian

Not clever enough yet
To lie, my mind
Trembles with an idea

In your language, brushing
Your cheek in Italian, languidly
My eyes intrigue themselves with rounder endings, while fingers

Caressed and caressing delve the sunlit shrine of your hair.
Why did you do this to me –
Seduce me into your foreign world
Of Dante's turning ovals?

I was happier with different metrics –
The orderly progression of feet and metres, curves of latitude
Or longitude, old rods and perches –
And all of the inches crawling obediently in English.

Now I am the clown of love:
Balancing your abundance
Is such tongue-tying trouble.
How can I keep your vowels up in the air

All at one time; how can I juggle
The Latin foreplay of words of love
In such a sumptuous foreign tongue?

The voluptuous ovals rise and fall
And I skip about under them all –
A prisoner beneath the loops and hoops; the toppling onslaught

Of all your charms and every rhyming line
Flung to curl down around me like a lasso –
Until I lie tangled up, wild with unspoken words for you

But choked – clotted up by my buttoned up
Tired old-fashioned Anglo-Saxon tongue –
The ovals and vowels bouncing and bobbing all about me.

## Polgeto, a village of Umbria

'The same landscape always repeated' – Vittorio Sereni

Thinking of the lazy green river
The watching hills, you revisit the Tiber valley
Village perched halfway up its sharpest mountain
The tenuous inhabitants called Contadini –
Cultivators – who live in a world above bubbles of traffic.

Quietness measured by the ticking
Of the hoe and mattock; the snips of pruning shears –
People with a knack for poverty, skilled in unprofitable
Schemes of seasons and weather, knowing by heart
The accords and discords, the inward song of weather-worship

Minds and bodies geared to survival, meticulous
In few choices – seed cast in spring, grain snatched in summer
Harvest; always-ancient song, and winter months of watching
A landscape resting, while the wind seethes and bellows
To itself – and shadows move as they do through leafless, grassless places.

Above the indifferent river of traffic exists a realm, a religion of doing without
Priests might only witness or whisper a tribute about –
And yet they were well fed on it; clearest eyes, shining hair
Movements supple and brisk, melodic shouting
Shuddering welcomes, a big hint of curiosity

In knowing smiles and their only treasure, or vice, even, was food
Celebrated and shared, with anyone, in frockless, ordained austerity.
So today in my own landscape I see their faces, nut brown
In whatever month; returning from vineyards or descending the olive groves
Their plain secret, poverty – filling those harvest sacks – and my astonishment

At the ongoing practice of a worn, well-grooved simplicity
Their boisterous acceptance of their lot; people from another time
Living above the traffic of ours, living for a different god
A god in a cob of corn, a god in a sack of wheat, a god in a glass
Of glinting wine – and remembered in my own shadowy wind

Trembling through feeble sunshine; memory climbing north
Through orderly fields and forests festive with light
The winding road equally eager to get there
As I drive my car higher into their sparkling spring
And I read their lofty, poppy-dotted fields and meadows
With an acute eye, borrowed from poverty; in years of auburn exile.

# Torte al testo

It was a lesson in cooking, or hugging
I'm not sure which, intermittent
Sizzling touches and damp kisses

Between her efforts as she rolled, lifted and pounded
The lump of dough on the table and shaped and rounded
And flattened it to fit on the flat stone

Glowing already on the fire.
An apron clinging against her perspiring nudity
She spat first on the stone's surface to see

If it was hot enough, then she lifted the stone
By its wooden handle and placed it to one side
And slapped dough hard down against it.

We watched the flat bread loaf browning slowly
Our faces theatrical in the flickering light
As our tongues relished more sweat and salt offered from both mouths

Our fingers foraging through harvests of hair
Our bellies young, quivering, a tautness barely touching
Her laughter with its sudden, bright tinkle

Broke the moment's tension before she said
Let's turn it round to the other side
There's no egg in this recipe, just salt and bicarbonate

So it will be crisper, almost like a southern pizza.
Later she cut the toasted flat loaf
Through the centre with a long knife

And then laid strips of translucent pink prosciutto
On one half and placed the other half over
To make the Umbrian Torta of unleavened bread

The prosciutto melting a little, odors of silky fat, warm
Like touches we shared and some more
Exploratory kisses, before eating the portions of evidence.

# August in Rome

Footsteps become a solitary dialogue
Echoing across the square
Where are the café tables?
Where is the everyday drama?

The gesticulations, slapping of foreheads
Fingers stabbing a cheek
Or rubbed together in the air –
Not one table, not one umbrella in evidence
No tipsy tinkling of glasses
No waves of resounding laughter –

Absolutely no one, not a soul whispers here
No one gazes from balconies
No one stares up at the crosses ablaze
The saints have lost their voice
The faithful have gone away.

A lone seagull, exile from Ostia
Circles the piazza, then flies back and forth
A pendulum set loose under the light
Of uninterrupted heaven, flight
Inviting envy, luring your eyes to follow

The fountain, despite its splendour
Splashes forlornly, a timepiece for silence.

Beneath the incredulous cries of the gull
You sense an inner discomfort, you, master
Of an empty, ancient square, complete with
An audience of statues, saints, gods and warriors
All unblinking, frozen in immortality, where stone
Anchors this silence, where stone is the only witness left.

An intruder in a world of bizarre silence
Or is this a dream, an illusion? –
See how your stride lengthens and lightens
And gravity is brushed to one side.
You are not quite a foreigner now
And you know why the city is empty in August

But the sudden disappearance
Of sound and voices shocks just the same
In the silence of absences, you see
The great marble urn at the top of one street
In another Viale, a fountain splashing for no one
And you miss your muse so distant, your Romanina
Idling on some blazing Liguria beach
Green eyes squinting at the sea, a swarthy Venus
Getting cocoa-brown all over
Shapely mythology ensconced in a tangerine bikini –
Here in streets that have lost their tongues
You grapple with a darkness of words

The threads of sentences where your protagonist
Is planning to steal a statue, the one
That crouches in Piazza Novona, a hand shielding
Eyes from a piece of mediocre architecture –
The story won't form, maybe you should
Head for the beach, shielding your eyes from the heat.

Time goes limp with silence
You feel like a puppy that's been left behind
Looking for a doorway that opens to woeful whining
Desultory splashes from a fountain fade behind
As you walk the narrow alleys down a shortcut
Under indifferent statues, a lone priest staring up at a dome
Then the last piazza crossed to your palazzo door –

You have a few more words for your story, you repeat
Them as you climb up the rising granite steps
Then the door and then
Into the cool gloom of your room.
From the window onto the piazza
You watch the seagull still swooping
Perching to circle on emperors' heads
And not one crust of bread to be seen anywhere.

At your little table you sit with an iced glass of water
Thinking a life of thoughts; vaporous islands
In the stream of being, clouds' shadows move
Across the square, thoughts' shadows
Also roam, here or there, in and out of curiosity's corners
Memory prowls again, far off or close to home
But is this home? Why are you here?
What does it serve? What is the purpose of this journey?

You begin to write down words, letters murmurings are louder
In the eerie silence, you are in another place now
You are with the great Roman poet
Trilussa, standing alone at last
At the very heart of the remarkable, empty city
Perfectly whole, found like an egg alone in an empty nest
The silence a reminder, an acceptance
Of solitude, like a swallow, you have returned
To the same perch; the islands of time turning onwards.

# Umbrian moon

Golden porthole through fathoms of blue up to heaven
Soaring circular Sphinx, slowing in midsummer-night air –
Sitting outside an Umbrian village bar
The withered harvester, Pino said

Gesturing crouched, with tumbler of ruby red –
God had set it all up for a game – *Un bel gioco* – and left –
Some trees he had liked to bunch together
Like sticks; rounder shapes when he played with hills;

Like we do with a trowel and cement –
After he dished up the mountains
Harvested the skies, scraped stars down
The ones he liked; others let go to drift like confetti out of His mind –

Here we are leaning back on this terraced ridge outside
One bulb above the door lights our world, behind
Green olives struggle to rise out of night-blue rock.
The evening seems to be waiting for Him

Moths may move but nothing much else
This July night will be still as it can immensely be
Seen and felt under stars' wheelbarrowing arcs of secrets
And the few clouds left, stopped in moonlight, after tumbling storms –

Only a mud-coloured congress of rats leap for the corn
Hung in long plaits from the gables
A curious sort of dance back and forth
As they continue to miss one claw's hook into the lowest cobs

Or give up eventually and seep away into shadows
To scratch at whatever habit comes to a rat's mind.

Midnight heavens are perfect, tomorrow will be fine, Pino says
Downing the dregs of blood red wine – and, he asks –
Why do these stars need us?
We look up there for Him, or for some answer

And of course it does not come –
We are not at the centre of things
We are the unfitted bits he left behind
The scattered parts of a jigsaw

He didn't explain, or try to finish – but then
When a star falls, like that slow torch there
Engraving a beautiful plume down the sky –
Wiping his mouth with a hand, the old man summarises –
I wonder always if it's a sigh still ending

Maybe a last tear of a thought; regret
In glittering sadness, which fell like a feather
Floating behind His steps
Passing from that time here, onwards.

# A fountain, casting moments of time

Tossing a line
To tug a thought back
The fountain forgives, again and again
What it casts it makes clear
It does not want back, rather it
Celebrates the beauty of endless replenishment.
You like that, that rhythmic expenditure, energy in giving.

In the beautiful movie
Of your youth, in a borrowed car
You have driven from salt-less Umbria
Following the spring-flowing Tiber
Down to sour old salty Rome, you'll
Take back some crusty roman loaves
And freeze half of them at home

The baker is in a bustling Saturday alley
Off Santa Maria in Trastevere –
You dally, pausing for a coffee beside
The prosperously belted fountain
Watched over by a bell tower, a dome –
Propped over heavenly columns and arches.

The marrow of time moves slowly
While you anticipate the warmer marrow
Of fresh baked bread, the 'midollo'
The middle, the Romans call it
Scooped out with your fingers
Alternated with a taste of crust
And chewed intensely with a child's guileful joy.

Humans converse like birds in Italy
More so Romans, bowing over a grappa or coffee
Hands weaving the air with embellishments –
Someone always breaks into song somewhere
And then sadly vanishes, words resonate
Hoarser from deeper ancient alleyways –
Spent emotions, ideas, convivial nonsense
Rising like doves and pigeons
Up stuccoed walls to sidestepping strips of sky;

What luxury of time to sit and listen and watch
You are breathless from excitedly
Walking to most of the favourite places
Under the décor of histories' worn backdrops, clocks and bells
Shedding languid dollops and droplets of time; lives of others
Resonate, where are they now; which street, which sky, where?
Which angle in different time? –
Your lost brethren
Wandering the earth, might go well, inked
Across a T-shirt – you'll stop and celebrate
Now with a gelato, watching a mob circle around a fountain

Do they see it, looking perplexed
Glancing sideways nervously at beauty?
There's no eye contact amongst them, no marriage with
A natural flow of moments, it's all about a mission
To uncertainty – to get it done and off to another –
Now is the moment for the self-portraits, selfless-selfies galore
So many faces last seen bobbing against a soon-to-be forgotten sky.

You thank inwardly a pretty girl, looking at you
From a balcony, she blows a smile from
A dimpled, olive-skinned face; tonight you'll
Remember her with a glass of Chianti
And a crust of chewy salty Roman bread –
The movie will continue, into another chapter as you imagine
Those wedding bells echoing off the walls of a Roman square
The wedding guests crowding out into a piazza
Resplendent with bouquets of red and white flowers –
Life has lent you this day, with a girl's smile
A fountain and a half-sung song – life, carelessly, tossing time back.

The Salt Wars between Pope Paul III and Perugia (1500s) regarding raised taxes for salt, deprived the Umbrians of salt – essential for curing meat, fish and baking bread. Umbrian bread is still baked without salt; a custom enforced by necessity that endured and became habit.

# Ruins

The temple has fallen
In love with the grass
Carved sections, half
Obscured, hint at more
The wind-whipped grass will tell no more

The glint in long running grass blades
Shares nothing; except the wind –
At this café table, cheese and olive
Taste different, in southern Sicily

The sheep's breath is still there, shared
With every olive's plump bitterness
And sharpens the tongue, the crumbling
Substance of cave-aged cheese

Is a foil for an olive's ripe discordancy.
Wine, black, smeared
Like youth's blood on your tongue and lips
Peeling back to a smile – guileful and demonic –

The sun our padrone – our straw-hatted gatekeeper
Lord of a sultry, pagan world.
The grass swishes
Over the fallen Doric column
A long ochre thigh undressed by the wind

Our hands flirt under the table
The sky is benign, watching us slyly
While fingers play ambitious roles
Moist from a long time ago –

More games, tumbling fun
Remembered between touches.

But today with you the swallows
Seem more alive, devilish even
As they turn and veer, chasing shadows of gods
Through the columns, in and out; light and dark of an epoch –

Last night we watched them, rise and flourish at midnight
Seen from shallow waters, gold dripping from our thighs
You splashed your cheeks with the gorgeous wetness
And drops ran down, molten between your breasts

For seconds, I saw the rocks, following
You down to the water, creeping behind like old lovers
Come to watch as the moon slipped
Away into clouds and your face darkened

And I could not see your mouth
Or what your eyes might have been saying.
In the dawn I strode up to the crest of the hill
And thought of you behind, sleeping still

And like a cypress or its perpendicular mind
I stood, looking down past broken columns
At ruins of a crimson sea and rocks
And the last image of you, in disarray
And spread in your limbs; tossed into paradise across the bed.

# Whether or not to love a tree

1.

You remember the first time
The cypresses in Tuscany delighted
So vividly with their smouldering green ellipticals
Heaven-sent spirals soaring in the heat
Sparkles spun in a rising curve
A swirling, voluptuous weave of needles
A top-to-bottom wobble, shapely in the wind, shimmering
Outlines erased then returned as if these trees were creatures
Suddenly wanting to step out of their shapes and dance.

And always, around the curve, heraldic, striking in plain sight
As one after the other, dutifully, in pairs
These cypresses ascend a hillside, such
A lot underlined yet still left unsayable
Likenesses only succeeding so far –
A shimmy in the wind
And threatening to step away
From their roots and twist free
And turn and turn
Gliding, naked of needles, across the field.

2.

Ireland, lough of the Celtic kings
Swans with wide, weighted wings
Glide above the Irish beeches
Sailing lazily into the silence
The lake glows, ruddy ripples at the edges
Water, still, withdrawn, contemplates

In the pause before the ending of light
Twilight trailing veils of shadow
Over the pinnacles of autumn-blooded leaves
Hushed, the whispering rushes, the low pools asleep
The time, the turning, is coming closer to deepest autumn.

Something vague, undefined glides
Above the placid surface
Not yet a shadow, while
The swans descend now
A tapestry of wings, floating down
In a bobbing white shroud and
A triggering thought, as secret
As a swallow, manoeuvres
Swooping to rest, hidden in the bemused mind.

3.

An idea? Or only a glimpse, or was it an echo of something?
As you follow the Umbrian path, long grass whispers
Around your calves – is a message reaching
From a forgotten season, still lingering about here?
Wind is faint above in the leaves
Like a distant conversation –
Leaves and twigs scissoring the reddened light –
Now back inside the walled garden, grinning
At a solemn, terse-lipped statue, Etruscan
Nobility dappled with wind-blown shadows
Tears of mist drip from blind, ancient eyes –

Clumps of oak leaves sway, pendulums of dark and light
Time dancing headlong down over grass –
Life could be like a fable sometimes
Should you love or not love a tree? –
A place on a foreshore?
A lake, in a view, serene? –
Or a corner in a park for forever more?

Then the joy of deciding nothing, finally
Leaning on a thought, on a pleasant memory
At peace without images, forgetting similes
For a little while, in this insistent, listening, silence.

# Far from the city

Like casualties touching, teaching each other
To limp better, we shared crutches until the end
You in your uncertain, trembling personality
Me chased by a fear
Of being finally alone with myself. We left the streets
Of dazzling geometry and struck camp

A great distance from the shimmering towers
Removed to where the sun flailed the earth with love
And made grapes and grain swell and ripen
And minds in the shade grow quiet.
But it did no good. You had been trained
Too well and had learnt to digest by heart
The music, designs of masters. You were the flute you played.

Like a jug of longing, you lived for the filling
And you absorbed the colour of every last cordial
Poured into the concave of your well-disguised want.
Time passed and I remained in the dry valley
At the place where the priest-corrupter took you away –
The hammering love gave me

Has worked another alchemy –
Instead of gold from mortal flesh it struck
Through until the crust of granite
Waiting inside me; a sour note for some, but the colour
And substance I found of sageness and restraint.
Now I do not seek you in dreams, where your body performs
Miracles; whether they be erotic or sometimes surreal.

I think only occasionally
On how you might be performing your rythmic rituals
The geography of your body a divine receptacle for dictates
Of others' minds, rhymes, alliterations or music.
Today in this midday landscape, I have eluded
The fear of being alone, for I turned
Quickly enough and snared its loathsome shadow.

This afternoon I squat in looms of darkness
A cave where we once made love well and much
A burrow under the sun's knuckled blast
A place that smells of basil and thyme after your departure
Remembered as a figure fading into the harshness of light.
I rest and listen to rythms of air in the rippled cool of twilight.
Here I have seen in a sun-planed landscape the heart
There is to be found; fragmented in scattered stones, the glint
That signals suddenly from granite. In the valley
Of abandonment where trees long dead
Writhe up for the sun, where rosemary and sage
Are the wind's best friends. I draw water from a well
Of the solitary – sustenance hauled dripping from buckets

Up from the resonating dark, astringent, pure
Uninformed water, a tacit companion for my tongue.
The syrup I sipped once and savoured faithfully
Was much too sweet for a mind prey to so many charms
Too tingling and fresh the pleasure, informed by the favoured
Ones; the verse-contrivers who pocketed my life
My memory, my time, so easily, with blurring spokes of rhyme.

# Islands and their ruins

1.

Ruins attract tourists, we flock
To see the bitter ending, arrive too late
To save the civilization
Written in rocks and rubble around our feet.

Looking, scrounging for omens scattered about us?
For proof of a god and heavenly vengeance?
His wrath spat out in rubble and stone.

Our footsteps barely brush the toenail
Of a dust blurred human tragedy,
The erosion here goes further, deeper
Than wind, the furrow's grasp of a plough
The stubborn goat's footprints
Climbing acres flooding plains can never reach.
The hazy signature we leave

Blows across a slighter surface
Over the mud-capped cries, those
Who had struggled to reach higher?

And died, hunched below the survival line.

2.

The island captures our hearts
We adopt it as our own
The lost crusoe in each of us, reaches for our part

Swaying in dreams of dreaming in a swinging hammock
We know we can see the whole wide world
Easily from here, freed from care, stress or blunt caresses

The crimson whiskey weed, a faster creature
Runs amock amongst the brittle tussock grasses
The wild lavender survives, still swings brightly
From the blown astray history of one lost farm, and

Now, we swing and rock and hug our adopted island
We love our dreaming hideout
We love the sway, the slow canter over time
The same returning to and fro, to and fro…

And then the realising, abruptly
Suddenly, swinging high up and then down
Of how we lost our way, so subtley, so smoothly
Surprisingly effortlessly and somehow without remembering
Which way we came – or how we swung so far away –
Or any swing left, known, unknown
Down or up or around, to get back home.

# Venus in Rome

We met in the ruins
Of someone else's civilisation

Under a dying warrior
You offered me a torn half of your sandwich

Around us the silent industry
Of thighs, calves, spears

And discus-throwing arms
Held their swaying moment.

A god, legless, armless, headless
Alive in absences, a plank of debris

Tossed up from shipwrecked artistic wreckage –
Once smooth, a curve of space

Today our staid facsimile.
Your eyes, sight for a divine statue

Thighs lithe on the heavy bench
Would find ample employment here

Lighter, amongst the sobering myths
Moving through the crowd of legends.

I'll walk you home, I said. Where do we go?

Near the Pantheon, you said, I live
Perched high up, with the pigeons…

In the dim twilight of the room
Amongst the noble marble remnants
A glimmer in her eyes, spoke of Venus.

# The bar on the Lungarno

In her green eyes
The tenderness of leaves
Brimming with light
On a hot afternoon, here
Under the trees – a waterfall of silence

A waiting stillness disturbed by a breeze.
I plunge thoughts across
The tables, into her gaze
Into her modesty and grace
The light on the river is heartbreaking

Held in abeyance
The palace windows shine, reflect
Echoes back from Florentine history
A glow above water floats, a pure note of light.
The Renaissance whispers
With the ripples of this river and lapping time.

Pages of memory flicker for a while
But despite all hope
And memory of better days
Many things are no longer the same
There will be no exchange of words –
She gets up and with a nod

Excuses herself from my gaze
And walks away
Under the linden trees
Until a wall of sudden sunlight
Swallows her up – I sit with my glass
Of Chianti vino and watch the water

Its simple need, function to go on flowing
Coursing under the bridges
Innocent and jocular it joyously glimmers.
I nurse the moments passed
And a perverse pleasure in her departure

A chance to finger, touch a lingering moment for love
Idle thoughts of her nakedness
Follow behind her billowing, sun-filled
White cotton dress, but I am free now
Fellow now with the restlessness of leaves

My palate relishes
The rich dark earth in this wine
A sip and a breeze of thoughts
A slow pure note of time
Skimming over the flows of the mind.

# Lunch in Napoli

We bounce around the city
In your mouse-sized Fiat
Buildings jostle above our roof window

As you drive like a minnow
Weaving through shoals of bigger fish.
We swish under the castle and we glimpse Vesuvius

Watching us, gleaming as we lurch
And straighten from a circle of staccato blurs
Neapolitans, captains of equestrian traffic swerving…

The woman singing on the radio
Has a voice you could squeeze like fruit
With its clotted lisps of mystery; a soft interrogative continuing…

Mouse parked, we grab our tickets and hustle through the aquarium
Hungry, in a hurry, we pass from fish dozing
Stacked from top to bottom in tanks, to the trattoria, to the view of the sea

From the terrace; a rolling cloth of flecked green crests.
We start to eat the cousins of our placid friends inside
'Fritto Misto' – nice, crisp outside,
Crustacean and battered fish heaped together

Prawn and whitebait, crab claw and John Dory
Fresh anchovies and oily sardines
Clothed in their crackling crust of bronze batter.

The breeze off the sea is a cool, short-lived relief
The slow, low waves shimmer and wriggle sequins
Like the 'frizzante' vino bianco we drink

Sipping in pauses of silence, from the bubbling liquid
Thinking of the touch of stretching fingers
Across our belly's and torso's welcoming flinch

The rub, 'Il freggare' of flesh in an apricot afternoon
Of tawny light, the cool harbour of our room
Waiting upstairs with its panorama;
Shutters flung wide toward Vesuvius.

# Venetian idyll

For Joseph Brodsky

Sole protagonist
Apprentice watcher

Graduate in Venetian Decembers
The vista clockwork
Of dozing clouds
Arches of sky
Bridges curving over time
No hands left to tell the time
Breath is the only measure
Where time ebbs, dithers
As it wastes itself – slow meadows of sky

Steadily undoing time, terracotta rooftops leaning
In along the canal, Venetian palaces
Stopped shoulder to shoulder
Ochre kneecaps and history in water, windows dream
Streaming images of sky
So much history, no time left

To think or add up, it's all here
Layer on layer, encrusted in brick dust
Eroded mouldings and flaking mortar
You daydream a question
What if I lived here?
Rock and stone and domes and crosses
All contrived for a home balanced on water?

Dipping your toes in time
A slowly moving mirroring of swells and currents
Seducing reflections of antiquity out to sea –
Marble, stone, brickwork
Rooftops, towers, domes, timeless arches
Do not sink, as light as the misty, floating air
They coast along coupled with rhythms of ripples
Down the canal, light is a painter
Daubing the tissues of water
Light spins under swirling moods of sky.

In front of my table several cats yawn
In a winter portrait of a feline family
And stretch and curl languidly
In a last pool of paling sunshine
Who needs museums? See
The people move from cathedral doors
Out along the weathered stone ways
With weather and history worn on their shoulders.

A pageant of morning shadows has crept back
Into lintels, architraves, walls and doors
Living, now hidden, in stone
To move again on a new Venetian day –
I sip the last of my cooled coffee
Watching a dazed sky drifting into purple exile
The waiter arrives, I order once more
His fugitive winter client, expert in migrating skies
Sipping another cappuccino to help diminish
The discomfort of doing nothing, not yet –

Numb? No, like the clouds I ponder
I savour, before I move, I stretch
In sympathy with the gang of cats
Who try to get up, but then simply cannot.

# The Naked Lunch

Her hips made a flick
A kind of signing off
A signature on spoken for property –
Then she rose to her knees
flexed on her haunches
And fell back into her muddle of limbs.

Her slow breathing fusing
A patch on my shoulder—-
I smooth her glistening hair
One finger crooked down a cheekbone
Her eyelids swoon, a flickering blue farewell
And she descends suddenly into sleep –

I think of her brown arms earlier
Filled with a snatched harvest of dark grapes
And those pink smudges among them;
Those tawny nipples jostling for space –
Her plump fruit bouncing just the same
About with those brighter reds
And ripe yellows of lemons
And an apple, escaping, rolling greenly away
As we leant together over the table –

Her giggles mimic the rippling of laughter
Before we rock to another ending
Slipping over the ledge, then sliding and
Landing like cats, on all four pads
Our tails up, our tongues pert, pink tips
Heading for the last course;
L'ultimo piatto, the final serving –
All the sweetness swirled
And consumed furiously in the next room –

Now our loose nakedness is knifed
By yellow diagonals, splashes of light
Flung down, and sideways
Through climbing Venetian slats –
And sounds of water lapping outside
Chopping rhythmically, methodically
Against the indifferent, moss-bearded walls.

The gondoliers, in their passages, cry up
To these palace windows bronzed by evening sun
Much higher than our own light-laced stone oblongs
Beyond the hired province of our four poster bed
And the dangling remnants of a kingdom's ceiling –

The rowers cries, their rhythms, drift through two vagrant lives –
And the flesh of the lemon, its essence continues continuing
Bouncing neat yellow echoes across the ceiling
Slicing out shapes the same as our dreaming mouths.

## Bologna

Lord I am golden from drinking
Your famous Lambrusco
I've stared deep into all of your Saints'
Eyes; gorgeous Cecilia, modest Mary Magdalen
Trailing threads of gold through their dresses;
The master Raphael painted, wondering blasphemously
If they were pink or golden on the other side.

Under slow golden light, under the arches
We ate tortellini, once fashioned after
The curls in a courtesan's navel, spied through a tavern keyhole
And made by the chef, a mesmerised voyeur –
From butter, oil, eggs, flour and water…

Now descending navels move about, creamily in my mouth
And my mind's lascivious tongue slips over the curve of a belly
Down to a lower unbuttoning of life
I imagine I'm lying with her on the edge of the bed
Knowing the hungry eye watches, blinking lust through a keyhole.

Now some of the sweet and nutty Parma ham
Streaked with creamy ribbons of fat
Draped over split purple figs
Covering their luscious ruby insides…
And cream spiced with truffles and Grana Padano
Slides in yellows over my tagliatelle –
I lift the strands, wrapped round my fork
As I anticipate, sniffing life's pungent source.

My tongue swims on through voluptuous textures
As I juggle a last prayer to Mary and Altissima Cecilia
And also to our carissimo friend, Master Raphael;
Please forgive me Maestro, for my ordinary images
Of what you have already made magnificiently famous…

Forgive me as well dear lord, my gastric promiscuity
Swallowing this platter of Emilian tortellini
Under your saintly alabaster gaze, under
Your patronage, under the drunken towers of our beloved Bologna.

# Exile – Or a crossroad in the realms of youth?

'Golden journeys, lost cities' – Derek Walcott

Over the glistening courtyard
Shadows glide on stone
Above the silence of stars
Around you, the silence of a ruin

Some unbroken windows glow
Under the gaze of the moon
But the narrative of slate, stone and rock
Has stopped – this is only what we know

The ruined tower might have whispered
It has nothing more to offer
Its day of war, defence and glory
Is over, only the ravens come
At dusk to nest in the yawning gaps

Only the clouds approach
As buoyant company and quietly go
Like moods drifting in and out of view
Like thoughts still too early yet to form –
High beyond the tower you watch

The stars enduring journey
Arching beyond all our impermanence
Beyond our bickering, a bright glimpse
Of eternity against the tyranny of the moment

Beyond cradle and grave
Beyond ruinous chaos
Beyond the foolish waste of our ravaged
Hills and fields, beyond even our lost god

Gravity shows its hand everywhere
We were not made to leap and fly
Beyond the calamity
Beyond this fallen stone and rock.
Now, back turned to the cobwebbed contours of time

And history, defeat or victory swallowed by mist and fog
It's time to walk on –back across the field
To the road you came on, shadows reaching
With someplace else to roam to

Your journey remains undefined
The moon, the dark, the ruin
Offer no advice; you were once from there
And still not yet from here

Should you have stayed behind?
The stars tell you, no – do not stop now –
Reason will come to reveal itself eventually
And there is not any sole spot in the world
Yet to call the chosen, hallowed place
Go on, go on – just go on your way
If the stars can find their way
And the dream, the idea, remains
Your exile will be a homecoming.

# Nardia

Without a calling for poverty
You learnt its crust
Young on the road
You tore at its marrow;

A sponge for wine, broth
And clarity, clearness
That forgave youth's electric clutter
Light that shone in things.

With little money, sparseness
Made beauty stark
Grace, naked a natural art
Eventually she was there

At the table in front of you
You knew little enough
But you sensed her beauty
Was a surprise, an unplanned gift?

Either that or divine intervention –
Years after, in streets of dreams
You still toss her kisses
Like pennies, flipping

Through the light and wind.

## Piazza delle Signoria: the square of the lords

Giambologna's rape of the Sabine women –
Much too beautiful – to introduce terror…
The launched symmetry, the woman

Suspended effortlessly above two men
Like a turning threesome; a circling team
Of Immortals – leaping into historical basketball.

A moment of nurtured stone, asserting
Marble is lighter than air, the sphere higher up
A figment of imagination, a resonance

You are meant to watch, later in recollection –
While her buttocks balance on the thrust of
A perpendicular line of male sinews and muscles…

Every time you cross the piazza, passing
The corner of the tower – rising stones like a prow
Cutting the light in half, you like to see

The same pigeon there, using Cosimo Medici's
Head as a lookout, a belvedere, the master
Of his steed and the Renaissance

Wears his fringe of dried excrement, undistracted
Urging his horse further into the history of cash and art.
And across in the shadows of the loggia

The three figures continue to leap
Like a fountain of flesh in joyous liberated stone –
Marble recurring in a fountain of ecstasy

Three leaps at a time in a pigeon's wingbeat of memory.

# Return to the hills and the Tuscan plain

Statues still stand
From a former life
Venus no longer smooth
Blotched with lichen
Apollo bruised with mould
Light and shade pass over black-lipped angels.

A gust of wind welcomes
Your return to this place
A trigger, a switch turns on
A whirlwind of leaves
A storm that quickly falls into stillness
Wind subdued, silence almost prevails except
For the faintly rustling store beneath your feet –

Surfacing voices, words from the past.
Rain has come and gone
Leaving puddles of sky, mirroring large
Dark birds swooping low down along the avenue
Real birds or do the images reflect your mood?
You remember the leaves, lazily
Gliding once, not like this animation

Images and leaves dancing wild and nameless –
The avenues of sky-climbing beech trees
Have miraculously waited, despite twenty years
Of ascent, despite your wandering absence –
From time to time bird talk
Bursting from naked branches – but no fluttering seen
Are these winged conversants real? Is this
Just static from another time in life?

The summits of cloud bear down
Passing over the crossroads of tree tops
Vaporous palaces, windows of memory, uncertain of an ending
Opening or closing, until a sound or a wavering
Image or a tinkling or an angle of light illuminates
And the moment jolts back into life, now – over there in dulled light
Daisies are chaste guardians before a faded Palladian villa
The perfect pond is still there but full of dead branches;
A forgotten black and white photograph; the Iron Gate
Still rings, grinds wide open to that long ago day

Now the fallen shutters are like rotting signposts
To one summer that nobody survived
The silence of shadows complicit, never confessing
Where she walked then or might walk now.

At the end of the avenue at the edge of the naked forest
The immense plain, the wind scrawled across the streaked sky
With its random rags of time, the flocks of flying dots
The ballets of swallows and beyond the glimmers
From a distant sea where you imagine winds
Herding freezing waves, rolling glimmers signalling to no one –
You look at the pattern of order below, crops
Planted, fields furrowed, Hawthorne hedgerows, somewhere a fox
On a verge of a ditch will sniff the air sensing out prey –
Bells of time ringing silently
But no one but yourself on the rise, hears

These slow rhythms, or a day of bells almost forgotten
A Sunday when you did not take that road
And with hope, descended slowly
Following her footsteps into another adventure
Sky and wind-chased leaves
Another fanfare, of life's wild greetings.

# Perpetual midday

'I am the muse and you are the poet' – Eugenio Montale

Is a shadow a coded message?
Motionless in the silence, in the waiting
Is there a secret explaining itself
An echo that may transcend human knowing
An echo that may transcend human knowing?

It's like the shadow is explaining
I knew you in a different time
In a different light, then –
Yes when we moved about together
I was the muse and you
Were the Ligurian poet – It's sad now

In this life of perpetual noon
To see you shadowless
You have become your muse
And moved beyond the chiaroscuro
Beyond the echo or the marriage or the union
Brother of ecstatic and brooding light.

# Central park and Columbus Avenue

Infinitely warm in your hand is the memory
Of her fingers entangled with yours
Wandering in a park painted with snow, windows
Like lit up alters, floating in all flanking views

The moonlit paths leading your eyes into the dark into the light
Through foliage shifting ahead, beneath the rising oblongs inlaid with gold
Christmas time is zipping up granite buildings into the blanketing sky.

She smiled around her turned up collar, her body
Plumply buttoned up with warmth that pulsed through
Her fingers into yours, promising more, the tepid hollow of air

Enclosed between your palms, a tryst not to be dislodged.
The snow skedaddled away from your feet
As you swung through the pinpricked tapestry of the dark

Pausing to kiss, both stroking for luck the bark of the old sycamore tree
Where somebody, Joe, had carved a heart for Mary
The wound now healed, a ripple of growth over the scar.

You sat for a while in moonlit profiles on the bench
In unconscious harmony with the sacred tree, you were
The stranger, she was the New York native, both of you nameless

And watchful aliens, paused halfway amongst the trails of trees.
You had met at Szabo's checkout counter; she with her tea, Earl Grey Twining
You with your shortbread biscuits; 'Is it time for tea?' you suggested benignly

She took you literally and by the waist; and, together arm in arm you walked
Into the streets under the stars, now both foreigners in love with the sky
In love with the golden outlines
Of passing strollers, their plumes of breath, no plans

To make, only the vague idea to walk contentedly together
For the length of a block
Before saying goodbye in front of her building, a looming moonlit
Citadel in the sky. After a hug before the foyer doors,
She decided in life's favour

And you both ascended, smiles faintly conspiratorial
In the mirror-walled lift, up past
The carpeted floors of nobody-talking-to-anyone-else floors
Except perhaps a blue-rinsed lady with a manicured pink dog

Until with a click and a buffeted shudder you were walking
Inside, across her abundant metres of parquet-patterned floor.

The park was a better backdrop to be with a mysterious stranger
She had said, pulling me out onto the terrace
Where we hugged, cosy in our wonderful warm strangeness
Under the same moon that patiently waiting
Had glazed the park to gold for us.

In the morning buoyed by bouts of love and tenderness
You slipped on your jeans and shirt to go down for milk and coffee
After shopping you returned to the foyer

A harvest of things in both hands as you walked into the lift then soundlessly
Ascending you remembered you had forgotten to remember
Her door number and her floor and her name you had never asked for.

# Cappuccino and almond cake

The past is never past
Floating in some rear-view mirror
Or sticky right there on the tip of my tongue –
Now it wobbles in a glass before my eyes
Or is under my hand or a folded napkin
Lingering, glowing, shining elsewhere


In many things – a glass of grappa, a circling whiff of wine –
Famously – in a provincial Frenchman's little biscuit.
Today I nibble an Italian almond biscuit
A Tuscan vineyard is there in the raison
An almond crumbling is like the faux resistance

Of your fingers; curling expectant on damask linen
Or absently stroking moist cotton, textures I remember
Touching – like the slow imprint of your kisses
The taste of lips, blackberry-burnished, ripened
From drinking robust country wine; summer drowsing thoughts
Vapour-drenched memory; I sip again the shape of your sigh, your thigh

Under damp, fine fabric; twisted torsos; tongues
Swimming in the liqueur of lust and kindness and
Strangeness; saliva a honey-sweet elixir in crowded mouths –
Who said the past is dead? I wipe my brow
The scent of memory lingers, makes a pale stain on my napkin

And my cup chatters back into its saucer.
In the little porthole of drained froth
Creamy streaks show my fortune has been told;
Moments to happen soon, circle in frothy caramels
A future swirled from random circumstances; scents

And flavours and textures –
Promising more light, more shade in an italian life.

# A smile in Italian

An immigrant
The other way round
I headed north instead
Of south, took my autumns northward
Toward Italy's timeworn springs.

Like love still out of step
I was a stranger there
Wandering ancient streets
Discovering walled villages
Hills of groves and vineyards
A homeless smile my signature
Strolling around a mountain in Umbria

Hideout for defrocked rebel priests.
For years those friends I had, long gone
Inspired me to set the table
For eight, my hats and coats flung over chairs
Made up the members of a Christmas feast;

A fantasized midnight-court of exiles, high above the Tiber
Steep inclines of misty nothingness, silent whiteness
Trees dusted with the earliest falls of snow
Sometimes I return to remember
Going back to walk those oak-wooded trails again

Or the high medieval streets, the Corso of Perugia
The Umbrian belvederes, cooling
Nooks and crannies of late September
Where Dante's wind was the coldest knife
And the winds had names of assassins.
This evening I pause in a Florentine

Square, Santo Spirito
The saint of the Holy Spirit
And watch the early evening splendour
The storming tapestry of fire
Raging above the church facade by Brunelleschi

Sipping again my preferred prosecco, watching the first ochre
Shadows shifting slowly, as usual at home across stones --
The fountain keeping to its laconic splash and
I observe the world of youth's pilgrims
Idling in the square, colours of other languages
Flowing around the surging fountain.

Was it the fading peach evening that kept us here?
Delaying our autumnal departures
Like swallows still up there, threading late after
Back and forth, an impetuous moon anchored still
To the glinting domes of the Renaissance

Or was it the ruthless elegance
Of the bow-like curve of the dome itself?
Early science, engineering, aesthetics
And hope – like the prow of a ship
Readied against the wildest, widest world
Of star-crossed sky? Or could it have been the cypresses

Cloaked in groomed sober greens?
Pilgrims of utmost fidelity, regularly
Crossing the crests, filing up the hillsides
Silently under the midday glare
Or beneath the gilding light of the faithful moon

Or was it in your heart

And your homeless smile
Something that longed to be lost
Happy in the tumult of humanity
On any street corner, content amongst
The eloquent to and fro of melodic salutations

A harmonious din of hellos, goodbyes
Singsong greetings in Italian
Under the leaves; those whimsical gliding pilgrims
All falling, circling through the soft din of remembered time
The shuddering of life, facades and portals
Saturated with slanted bars of golden light

Where autumn
Wherever it is
And whenever it is
Speaks its time and place and
Its golden measure
In ochred accents, verse and words of Italian.

# The little waves

They sense you –yes it is you –
Your footprints have returned.
A storm moves darkly over, appears to notice
Then goes quickly, silently back
Drifting onwards out to sea –
The silence is just the same
Severed by toppling, tinkling fractures of water.

The breeze whispers
But not for sharing
Only the splashes confess
In their ancient, rhythmic language
The day when she left the island

The rocks cast shadows
Over the water and swept down into waves
When she rowed away
Her oars dipping through buoyant shadows
Over the sinuous, monotonous kelp
And the little craft became a dot, drifting out
Swallowed in the glow of a thirsting sea.

This summer, years after, I have returned
To this bay alone, the whispering roman pines
And the rickety, sun-blistered house – simply for the love of memory –
Nothing has changed and there are no signs of squatters or claimants
The glass panes are still mostly missing
The bare rooms as before, but for one narrow bed, boards
Gleaming clean with a clustered glowing of sunshine.

Nothing to confess of former presences
The unlocked door still creaking back and forth
Swinging to some bird-bickering nonsense – then walking
Down the sand, diving in, swimming again
Head back, drifting over the shallows, savouring the sky again
New and old memory swirling above clear sands
Her milk-green nakedness suddenly showing itself, wavering
Like curvaceous human kelp –I scoop up a palm full of water
And taste again those cool, sweet lips and salty fingertips

And remember moments enjoying the smiles in her curious eyes
And the gulls seemed to have read my sentiments
With crowding cries in the swaying of unspoken moments
As I squatted on haunches and stared
Out at the same horizon, sea simmering
Along a bronze curve that holds
No tracks, no wakes, no indications
Of beginnings or endings.

A long wake drifts and the island is well behind you now
Coming around the headland
You will see her once again
Sitting, legs crossed, in her myth, in your dream
On that high rock or the other even bigger one
Combing out wet hair with her fingertips
And as the sea resists the bow, the old churning returning
From there and then, you look back to her, composed
Again in her secret, lingering history

Her frailty blending into stone
And gulls cries flake and glide down like
Skies' fragments of drifting, drizzling time –
And even as you reach the mainland

You can still taste
Those fingertips, those lips, even
Though she is really gone
Truly gone, fading beyond
Even your memories' reach.

# Remembering Lerici

Rhythmic murmuring of seashells
The echoes of crunching waves
The curves of falling seawater –
Like everything that vanishes
Everything starts like a wave

Rising then peaking, gathering momentum
Then at the ordained moment the crest
Falls over eloquently – Oh if we could only
Escape time, escape the falling, the sliding
Become invisible, freed, weightless, infinitely drifting –

And suddenly has your heart set sail
Like a quavering wave
Gone with your untranslatable smile
While here, ankles deep in grit and foam
The roars gnaw at me
Stuck with my miserly hope
On a plaintive, complaining shore

And what has become a colder sun
Lethargic, even paler still in veils of haze –
Alone again with the ordained waves
The shifting, ticking pebbles
With the quizzical murmuring – of seashells
And the bounty of whispers you gave away.

# Driftwood

In memory of Marianne Moore

Formed from water's lacerations
We were Love's driftwood
Each from so far away
Shaped by life's lathes
We drifted down desolate coasts

The cracking of ice
The seagull's lost cries
Time tossed again and again
Against an unknown shore, some unnamed beach
Floating through roars and cries
From a sea of sweeping loneliness –

How many wet, moonlit rocks
Do you remember?
How many swirls of sequins gliding
Onward, can I? –
Our twisted shapes
Our twisted natures
Kindred distortions
Arabesques of misfortune
Found some dawning harmony –

Pieces of the same wind-blown puzzle
Whitened, dry, whittled and weathered
We drifted now up onto the land
Moved ahead with monumental skies
Lived alongside the pageants of weather
Heading, this time, for one more journey
One more story, misfits together, painted into the distance
Horizons getting closer, both serenely afloat and drifting.

# A room fallen asleep

In memory of Eugenio Montale

Outside the snowflakes swirl
Toward another destiny
Here no longer
Does a poet's shadow attempt
To fit in. Where is the wearer?
The former shaper of this fading outline?

Is the soul a tenant
Now flown, to perch
Once more in a different dwelling?
The glass beside the bed
Is empty, the dose of life, since swallowed?

Silence is this brimming emptiness
Once a fullness of time. Will someone weep
When stumbling in and they discover
All these sleeping things?

Everything in this room
That served a purpose
Is mute, nothing belongs
Only the last light lovingly clings

And forgotten in a corner;
A candle sobbing shadows.

# In memory of Basil

Certain light in Art Deco lifts
Flatters my face
The mirror and I
Repeat the journey to make sure.

Dimly in the foreground
Of the café I name Paris
(Worth a mass)
I still decline to age.

Youth clings to my complexion
Like an anxious fly
My insides refuse to rot
Perhaps red wine

Has preserved me
For one more bon mot.
Sipping the froth of a cappuccino
I remember his word agog

Balanced, surfing on foam

And dabble a bit with Bunting's
Line about cunning flies
Examining cake – (academics nibbling
On a poet's life?) – Elsewhere tables

And chairs round me creak and submit

To existential meaning;
People without wings or eloquence
Who lean lovingly over chocolate éclairs –
Not cunning, just hungry

Longing for solace; reading pastry with both hands.

# Bells I can remember – Venice

A different, strident sound today
Exuberant and echoing
Like rising hearts of blazing waves.
Years ago behind the Venetian fog
I hoped there were angels, hovering there
Behind dull, muffled December days

The sun vagrant behind looming, vague
Outlines of towers and domes;
Contemplative profiles in that soup of grey air
Lights in windows over canals
Seemed to be floating lanterns
Leading, intriguing me on – here I walked where

He had walked along his tidemarks

But never crossed him; I with my poet's cloak
Black Sicilian sombrero, tapping
My unconvinced cane – where he had scurried
In his old raincoat and indifferent cap, scavenging
For words – The depth of hollowness in the fog
Did not echo but the stones endured a new poem

As I muttered it under my breath – over and over.
I dread to think if he had ever heard me
And then reversed his tracks down another alley
Escaping my ongoing, doddering meter.
Today a vastly different light, a sluggish mood of evening sky
And I walk through shadows of my old self

Plainly dressed now as mister-nobody-knows man
Without a Borsalino hat or cloak to climb the steps of the Rialto
There in any old faded shirt, I remember his musing
About foggy Venice in winter;
'Like Greta Garbo on her side, swimming.'

Even though spring has almost thawed
I won't follow her lazy sidestroke, naked or dressed
Diving below to reach out for her in the streams of blue cold.

# Praying aloud

Returned – once more to the view –
Those distant mourners
Mountains of Connemara – unchanged
Beautiful and immensely morose.
The sea is smashing its pebbles, again, again
Vigour and malice churning about in waves
Gaelic an ancient language; parchments of accents in the wind.

Down in an empty church
I found you – praying aloud –
Had love gone wrong for you? –
Here in the west of Ireland; her
Seesawing graveyards of stone;
Her clouds forever unfurling over

The sea and the skies' blue hope –
Your prayer pleading out to mayhem.
Today the sea's music falls crisply on freezing beaches
Groans of deeper realms surfacing in between;
Was there too much magic between us? –
You vanished with an accountant

Much safer, anyway – I delayed, and then drifted away.

Sometimes in the brightening hour
You are dawn's shapely child
Emerging veiled in grey-pink gauze, and
I hear your prayers between those waves
And waves here of my own, as light lifts its veil
And a song flows over Galway, mourning that prayer that day.

# The man in the Academia

In memory of Joseph Brodsky

It is autumn – not quite as sure of itself as winter
But gusty enough, driven on that eventual course –
The colonnades recurring like lace over water
The canal a mirror flowing with browns

A spillway for running yellows and greens…
In the history of sky-tinged insights here
The guest writers have already packed up and gone
Taking their rumpled pages, glimpses and recollections

Back to native lands elsewhere. But there is one
Who always returns; a watcher of winters
A poet drawn to last year's watermarks
Come to note the wind's watery glints and gather the floating residuals…

He has booked again into memory – the same well-grooved room
A door in the Pensione with bed, a desk and finally the window
Leaning over the canal – his mind is already inclined forward
Into the season he likes, his smile is readying to write, soon

He puts back on the cloth of this season taking his first morning stroll
Glad to rediscover the colours he remembered curling down the canal
He takes the lesser-known alleyways to reach the old marketplace
To reread the prices of fish chiselled into maritime history

Then steps over one of the impeccable, unfamous arches
Enjoying its sleeping dream of a shadow below
And just twenty steps past a committee of grey
Circumspect cats – he gets to the little café where he sits beneath the faded

Stripes of the awning and watching the tactile glide of water –
Sipping the acceptable drug of coffee and blowing his chains
Of unacceptable smoke – cordite-blue spumes
Into glass-transparent Venetian air.
There is no news of the other world here

There are no lists to scrunch up or to scribble here
No better or worse students, no appraisals
No nurturing of young febrile minds to sort out here
He sits with his own mind and his jittery companions; coffee

His conscience and his cigarettes, watching the subtle
Slower light work its glow over things; seesawing textures
On water, the bright barbs spun on angles of bricks, the curved warm cheeks
Of terracotta – a Russian now sitting inside an American professor
A poet awake now inside an expatriate, an exile
Anchored forever inside an exile
And nothing about in the sky or on land to notice
Any of this, the canal flows as usual
The seabirds are circling the zone; the domes doze, doped with blueness
The gulls now quiet – are prospecting – up and down those ochre curves –

The browns and softer blues have it – dominating
The flow of quietness and in a gentle daze
A geared lethargy – he begins to write
The first movements – wriggles of watermarks arriving –

Lines lapping recollections – first words wavering in his mind.

# Venice, summer ends

Water plays whimsical knave
With marble lace, freed it ripples
Like memory; arches wobble
As if doing a samba out to sea

A launch cuts through a picture
Of stone and sky, churns colours
Its wake a pulverization of beauty
The coiling streets are ribbons to mystery

Intrigued you follow them into the ancient marrow
Of rust brick and grey stone; tight, sentinel circles
Until you reach water again; recycling
Landscapes you vaguely remember

From museums of recollections, melancholy of cathedrals –
You glimpse in the drift of the canal
A flowing depiction from a palette of squiggles;
Yellows, russets, ruby reds, crimson tears

Stretch, rippling from Titian – the art will not last
The landscape turns over like a page
Impatient to slide downstream;
The fluted chimneys, the dozing domes

The snoozing shutters, the city sleeps
At the edge of depiction, like a noble elder
With one eye open on a wilful child
That won't stop playing with a hoop of light.

You plough toward the staring facades
Old-timers lined up in the sun
Shadows withdrawn, slinking under bridges
As you speed on past; decay barely breathes the air here

But the water is still young; splashing bright anarchy.

# Acknowledgements

*The Canberra Times*
*Overland*
*Contrappasso*
*The Australian Love Poetry Anthology*
*The Canberra Poetry Anthology*
*The Henry Kendall Anthology*
*Five Bells*
*The Irish Centre For Poetry Studies Anthology*
*The Independent Media Ireland*
*The Sigh Press Florence, Italy*
*Poets Corner New York*
*Quadrant*

www.ingramcontent.com/pod-product-compliance
Lightning Source LLC
Chambersburg PA
CBHW050419120526
44590CB00015B/2020